TABLE OF CONTENTS

ACKNOWLEDGEMENTS

The Story of Manor is reproduced in this book as it was originally written, except for the errata of Mrs. H. D. Patterson. The errors Mrs. Patterson found on pages 14, 33, and 51 have been corrected.

Appreciation is extended to the following people who provided invaluable contributions to the completion of this book. Thank you to Philip Pietrusza, Jr. for providing computer support and to Melinda Pietrusza for her Hollyhocks artwork. For stories, pictures, and oral histories we are grateful to Avis Altman, Carl Beretta, Mark Bradley, Guido Ciccarelli, Marian Eisaman, Helen Hopkinson, Carl Huszar, Gretchen Lauffer, Jane Liebdzinski, Karyl Nicholas, Bill Oblak, Joanne O'Bryan, Judy Rebich, Joanne Schneider, Vera Shale, Jack Sproat, Pat Stawicki, Tom Steeley, George Valmassoni, Virginia Wahl, Mary Ann Walter and Cil and Chuck Wergin. A special thanks is extended to Carla Thompson and Carol Richardson for formatting the index and to Nina Kemps, Nancy Miller, and Stephanie Brooks for assisting with the final editing.

MANOR
Pennsylvania

A Place in History

Editors

Gail Martz Noll
Dorothy Y. Miller
James Thompson

Committee Chairperson

Phylis Pietrusza Levino

Committee Members

Marlene Cox	Rexford Cox
Paul Dzendzel	Tom Haubrich
Dick Hauser	Helen Hauser
George Heasley	Al Horsmon
Vivian Horsmon	Audrey Kozain
Donna Nedley	Betty Nicholson
Don Nicholson	Loretta Schroder
Helen Sowash	Enid Walter
Linda Whitehead	Wayne Whitehead

Word Association PUBLISHERS

Tarentum, Pennsylvania

ISBN: 1-59571-108-2
Library of Congress Control Number: 2005938228

Word Association Publishers
205 5th Avenue
Tarentum, Pennsylvania 15084
www.wordassociation.com

Cover photograph by J. R. Downs courtesy Pittsburgh Tribune-Review.

Funds for the printing and publishing of this book have been possible by the families of Cora Hoyer and Edward Miller.

Proceeds for the sale of this book will benefit a special project for Manor Public Library.

FOREWORD

Over the past several years, several attempts have been made to have the original *1976 Story of Manor (1783-1940)* republished. The copies that are in the Manor Public Library for reference use are requested frequently. New Manor residents who have purchased an older home are interested in obtaining its history. Others who have moved from Manor come to the library to research family history.

I contacted Phylis Pietrusa-Levino, who was chair of the committee for the 1976 book, to help with this republishing of the book. She agreed to take on the project. Gail Noll, a native Manor resident, who was volunteering in the library and personally knew many people in town agreed to help. Her knowledge added a catalyst to our effort.

The three of us first met in my home where we outlined a plan. Gail then set up a committee of interested people. Jim Thompson joined the group of editors, and with his wife, Carla, added to the mix. It was decided that the original 1976 book would be the first section of the 2005 book. Additions to the original stories would be inserted within this section. The pages would be numbered by using the letters a, b, c, etc. Additional stories of Manor collected from long-time residents would be in the second section of the book. The final section would focus on the women of Manor and their organizations.

The book committee, comprised of twenty-two members, met for the first time on May 23, 2005 at Manor Public Library. The committee set a deadline for the book to be completed and published before Christmas. Helen Sowash has been an invaluable source of information. I think of her as a walking history book of Manor. Her help and factual support cannot be surpassed.

The history of Manor reflects the decline of the railroad, small family farms and businesses, and the decline of the mining industry. Manor's story recounts love, pain, and trials of individuals who lived through those evolving days. A small piece of Manor's pulse can be felt in their stories.

Other struggles that were a part of Manor history are: children getting an education in a primitive school building, men facing dangers in a mine, and women providing unselfishly for their families while making time for culture. All are remembered in this book.

For many of you who hold this book in your hands, Manor is a warm memory of home, and home is where your history begins.

By Dorothy Y. Miller

INTRODUCTION TO THE 1976 STORY OF MANOR

The Story of Manor, Pennsylvania (1783-1940), was a product of the celebration of our country's bicentennial in 1976. Looking back through those 29 years, many things escape my memory, but I remember how it all came about. In 1975, I was in the Westmoreland County Court House in Greensburg, when I ran into Hazel Adams whom I knew from the Westmoreland County Historical Society. Hazel was chairman for the County's Bicentennial Committee and was looking for people to begin local committees. She asked if I would be willing to set up a committee in Manor. She gave me the general guidelines, which I then presented to Manor Borough Council. Council agreed to involve the community in the celebration. The Manor Bicentennial Committee was formed in 1975 by proclamation of Manor Borough Council, Westmoreland County Commissioners, and the National Bicentennial Committee. I agreed to be committee chairman.

OFFICIALLY RECOGNIZED -- Russell Crise and Westmoreland County Members of Manor Bicentennial Association Commissioner Robert Shivey. Recognition hold their flag and certificate which they was received from American Revolution received on becoming an official Bicentennial Administration (ARBA). The bicentennial group. From left are Nancy official flag raising ceremony will be held Otto, publicity coordinator; Phyllis 4:30 p.m. Tuesday, Nov. 25. The public is Pietrusza, chairman; Alice Davis, invited to attend. representing Manor Woman's Club: Mayor (Standard-Observer Photo)

Article Courtesy – November 22,1975 Standard Observer

PHYLIS PIETRUSZA, 1976 MANOR BICENTENNIAL CHAIRPERSON

The national guidelines suggested an event be planned for every month, and that events be given a bicentennial theme. Among the most memorable was the painting of murals on the walls of Manor School. Manor PTA President, Pat Stawicki, and Principal, Norman Pezze, organized a group of parents, teachers and volunteers to paint all of the walls in the school with bicentennial themes. The walls were coated with polymer, and the murals were still in excellent condition when the school closed in 1990. The painting of murals in the school was an event that attracted the attention of local newspapers and television stations.

The postmaster gave permission to hold a street fair in the post office parking lot and provided electricity when it was needed. The Scheuerle family put us in contact with the musicians' union, which donated a band to present a concert in the post office lot. The concert audience reached crowd proportions, spilling over in the streets and into the bank parking lot. The churches held a Sunrise Service, and the Manor children painted the subway under the railroad tracks. The junior firemen, under the direction of Babe Brigode, painted all the fire hydrants in town red, white, and blue. The November event was a Thanksgiving dinner at the American Legion and in December a giant Christmas tree was set up in the Borough parking area by the firemen.

GEORGE Y. HEASLEY

The national guidelines stressed that each community should do something that would be lasting. The Naley and the Caldwell families were asked to share information about the book they were trying to write. A book would be a lasting gift to the community. George Y. Heasley, a graphic editor for Westinghouse, volunteered to get the book project started. George guided this work through a busy schedule for his shop, and managed to get it done for a nominal cost. All 635 copies of the 1976 book were sold before they left the plant, and the Committee had money to pay Westinghouse.

The 1976 book project led to the book you now hold in your hands. *Manor, Pennsylvania, A Place in History* was done by updating the bicentennial book with additions, corrections, and new stories told by Manor's senior citizens. Some of these oral histories cover three, four, and even five generations of families making Manor's history worth preserving. Congratulate those who have contributed to this effort, for it is, indeed, a present for the future.

BOB CUPP, WRITER FOR THE TRIBUNE REVIEW, VISITS THE MANOR BOOK COMMITTEE AT ITS JULY 2005 WORKING SESSION AT THE LIBRARY

By Phylis Pietrusza-Levino

The Story of
MANOR
Pennsylvania
(1783-1940)

U.S.A. Bicentennial Year 1976

The Story of
MANOR
Pennsylvania
(1783-1940)

U.S.A. Bicentennial Year 1976

MANOR BOROUGH
MANOR, PENNSYLVANIA

TO MANOR BOROUGH COUNCIL, who, in this year of 1976, were instrumental in getting the Bicentennial program in our community off to a good start,

TO THE ORGANIZATIONS in our community, whose cooperation in promoting this project was very helpful,

TO THOSE INDIVIDUALS who contributed in so many ways, a well deserved thanks to all.

COMMITTEE

CHAIRPERSON . . . . Phylis Pietrusza
COMMITTEE . . . . Mrs. Alice Davis
                                           Mrs. Nancy Otto
MAYOR. . . . . Russell Crise
SECRETARY . . . . Mrs. Alice Davis
TREASURER . . . . Miss Thelma Lessig
PICTURE & STORY EDITORS . . . . Mr. & Mrs. Wayne Caldwell
MANUSCRIPT TYPISTS . . . . John Naley and
                                           Miss Thelma Lessig
GRAPHIC EDITOR . . . . George Y. Heasley

CONTENTS

FOREWORD

To know nothing of the past, is to understand little of the present, and to have only a vague conception of what lies ahead.

The purpose of the Bicentennial year is to rekindle memories of the past and preserve them for the future.

In this book, a small group of interested people have made an attempt to record the beginning years of Manor, with material solicited from spirited citizens scattered throughout the country.

All copy and photographs submitted for reproduction were screened to provide the most accurate and authentic story of the time period this book portrays.

We owe a debt of thanks to the many contributors, without whom this book would not have been possible, and much of the history of our town might have been lost forever.

To all who read this book, may you find real enjoyment looking back on a colorful bygone era; with further hope that the contents herein will provide an even richer experience for future generations.

HISTORY OF PENNSYLVANIA

William Penn received a large grant of land from King Charles II about the year 1681. This grant was made in payment of a debt owed by King Charles II to William Penn's father. This grant of land extended from the Delaware River to the Ohio River.

Penn, being a wealthy man sat down and made treaties with the Delaware Indians here and paid them fairly for the land. This region was settled fast, mostly by Germans, some Scotch and Irish, who were never molested by the Indians.

In later years, frontier men, scouts, and explorers were making their way across the Allegheny Mountains; some of them were from Eastern Pennsylvania and others came from the Virginia Colony. Among those early frontier men were John Fraser, George Croghan, William Trent, Christopher Gist, and Hugh Parker.

The Ohio Company was formed in Virginia and sent scouts to this region. About 1754, Trent, Gist, Fraser, and Ward began construction of a small fort on the Ohio which they called Fort Prince George. The French had made great inroads along the St. Lawrence River and down the Ohio and there Commander Contrecoeur took this fort in late 1754. The French rebuilt this fort and called it Fort Duquesne in 1754. Later, the English built forts at Bedford, Ligonier, and also Fort Necessity.

General Braddock was sent out from the Virginia Colony to lead an attack on Fort Duquesne. He followed a path along the Potomac River to Willis Creek, later to become Cumberland, Maryland and then went west along a route that later became the Old National Pike.

George Washington accompanied Braddock on part of the trip. Braddock never made it to Fort Duquesne. At a point west of Turtle Creek on the flat strip of land between the river and surrounding bluffs, he was met by a large force of French and Indians; and was severely defeated. Braddock was mortally wounded here and in the retreat died, several days later, near Fort Necessity and was buried there.

This battle was fought at the present site of the Edgar Thomson Steel Works. In the summer of 1758, Forbes cut out a new path along the Raystown branch and the route which was later called the Forbes Road.

In September of 1758, Major Grant made an attack on Fort Duquesne but was repulsed. Later that year, Forbes found Fort Duquesne abandoned and burning. In 1759, General Stanwix arrived and ordered Engineer Harry Gordon to rebuild a new fort. By 1761 a new fort had been constructed and called Fort Pitt. The Indians were friendly with the French due to their association with trading and land policies. Fort Ligonier was under siege and attacked but the fort never fell; Fort Necessity also was overrun and abandoned for a time.

By 1763 Pontiac, whose tribe was located along the Great Lakes was able to unite most of the Indian tribes, this being called Pontiac's Conspiracy. All the forts were under siege at this time, Fort Erie, Fort LeBeouf, Fort Pitt, Fort Venange, Fort Ligonier, and others. Col. Bouquet, a professional soldier, having arrived earlier in Eastern Pennsylvania, was chosen to lead a force west to break this Indian siege. They had a large force of men and wagons and pack horses when they left Fort Bedford. When they arrived at Fort Ligonier, Bouquet decided to leave the wagons behind and travel ahead with only pack horses, of which they had 350. Bouquet wanted to travel west to reach Turtle Creek and the Braddock vicinity after nightfall, so as not to be observed, because he considered this spot to be the most dangerous.

By August 5, 1763, Bouquet had not yet reached Bushy Run Creek. Out of nowhere, shots were being fired. They were on higher ground here and quickly assembled all the pack horses in the center of the circle and the troops were on the perimeter. Bouquet's troops were completely surrounded and water was not close. They fought all day till dark; some firing continued through the night. Since 350 pack horses require giant amounts of water, Bouquet was forced to send squads to replenish the water.

Then on the morning of August 6, 1763, Bouquet and his forces, still surrounded, had to sit down with his second-in-command, Major Campbell, to devise a plan as they faced complete destruction. Bouquet, being a professional soldier came up with his plan; a feigned retreat and pincher movement. When the several companies put the retreat in motion, the Indians saw this and came out more in the open. Those companies moved far enough to the rear so as not to be observed and then fanned out to both sides to complete the pincher movement. Whenever the pincher movement was about complete, Bouquet's men blasted the Indians from the front and both sides. The Indians being stunned thought giant reinforcements had arrived and fled the field. The Indians on the other side of the circle, seeing what happened, fled the field also. Thus, Bouquet, with his plan turned certain defeat into the most decisive victory fought on Pennsylvania soil. Bouquet moved on August 6th, 1763 to Bushy Run Creek where they stopped to replenish their whole water supply. They later moved through that Turtle Creek-Braddock strip with only a few shots fired. Bouquet arrived at Fort Pitt in August, 1763, with all their supplies. This was practically the end of the Indian siege and Pontiac's conspiracy. The Indians moved west of the Ohio River after this battle, and the few settlers were more secure and many settlers were able to move here from the east. Bouquet received high acclaim for the most decisive victory in eastern Pennsylvania, and in later years he received the same high acclaim in the Halls of London.

Bushy Run Battlefield, located in Penn Township at the present time, was carved out of four surrounding townships, namely: Hempfield, Franklin, Salem, and North Huntingdon in 1855. This land was part of the Denmark-Manor grant of land; later part of Penn Township, and after the railroad was put through in 1852, was called Manor Station. Still later in the year of 1890, it was incorporated as Manor Borough.

HISTORY OF MANOR

It is doubtful whether any section of the United States has a more interesting history than South Western Pennsylvania, which embraces the County of Westmoreland. There were primarily two reasons for the settlers to come to this section: the first was a settlement of the French on the Saint Lawrence River in the first half of the seventeenth century; second, was the formation of the Ohio Company in Virginia which was composed of Virginia Capitalists. The French desired to expand their fur trade. When the Ohio Company learned of the French Scouts that were being sent out in the section now known as South Western Pennsylvania, the company immediately started securing and diverting the fur trade with the Indians from the French. The first English speaking explorer to traverse South Western part of Pennsylvania was Christopher Gist. From that time on the English speaking people began settling in the southern part of Pennsylvania.

For a third of a century following its colonization, the South Western part of Pennsylvania was constantly engaged in warfare; with the Indians, the French, and later with the English in the Revolutionary War. In addition, the early settlers had to struggle with the wilderness, subdue and make suitable for their habitation.

Three counties had been formed by William Penn in Pennsylvania in the year 1682; Philadelphia, Buck, and Chester, or the Quaker Counties. In 1729, Lancaster County was formed, then York County was formed twenty years later and in 1750 Cumberland County. Westmoreland County was then located in Cumberland County. Arthur Saint Clair aroused the people in South Western Pennsylvania to set forth petitions to organize their own county. On February 26th, 1773, Governor Richard Penn signed the bills forming Westmoreland County.

One section of Westmoreland County was known as Denmark Manor; one of the Manors or Estates procured from the heirs of William Penn. This was a grain producing section in the last decade of the 18th century and the first half of the 19th century. In fact, at this time the State of Pennsylvania was the only state in the newly formed Union that produced more grain than its inhabitants could use.

The settlers of Denmark Manor were Pennsylvania Dutch. These Dutch settlers along the Brush Creek began having trouble with the Indians; so Fort Walthour was built. One may correctly call Fort Walthour a blockhouse, since it was built by the neighboring farmers for temporary safety. For weeks at a time the settlers would spend the night in the fort and would go to their fields to labor in the day time. In 1783, Stofel Walthour, a Dutch farmer, on whose land the Fort had been built, erected a grist mill. Farmers came from miles around to this section of the country to have their grain ground.

The account of the Willards being killed at Fort Walthour is well authenticated and is as follows: Captain Willard, his daughter, and two sons were working in the fields near the Fort, on a morning in 1788, when a band of Indians appeared and began firing on them. The Willards ran towards the blockhouse or fort but the daughter was overtaken. The father and his sons put up a fight, but near the fort the father was shot at close range by one of the Indians. The Indian who ran up to Captain Willard and was about to scalp him, was hit by a shot from the fort. The injured Indian lay in hiding for three days but finally escaped. Years later when peace had been restored in this section, inquires were made among the members of the Delaware Tribe, of which the injured Indian had been a member. The Indian assured the settlers that Davy a sub-chief missing since the slaying of the Willards had never returned to the tribe.

For a number of years Fort Walthour and the Walthour farm house were the only buildings in the section of Denmark Manor, known as Manor. In the latter part of the 18th century and the early part of the 19th century more Dutch farmers started settling in the Manor Valley because of the rich farm land, and also the coming of the railroad.

In 1836 when there was talk of building a railroad from Philadelphia to Pittsburgh, the people of Westmoreland County expressed a desire for the road to run through their county and a meeting was held to this effect in Greensburg on April 19th, 1836. On April 13th, 1846, ten years later, the Pennsylvania Railroad Company was chartered and the first locomotive entered Westmoreland County from the west, that is, from Pittsburgh in the year 1852. It had been built in the east and was taken to Pittsburgh in pieces on canal boats and there it was assembled for use. On its trip from Pittsburgh, it arrived at Radebaugh Station on Monday, July 5th, 1852. People came from miles to see it because most of them had never seen an engine. Many of the settlers from Manor were there to study the engine with great interest. On Thursday, July 15th, trains began to run regularly from Radebaugh to Pittsburgh and back.

Coal was a valuable product in Westmoreland County in the 19th century. The Penns were aware that the South Western part of Pennsylvania was rich in coal fields. This may be seen by a letter from Thomas Penn in London, dated May 12th, 1769, to the Governor John Penn. "I would not engross all the coal hills, but rather leave the greater part to others who may work them." In 1784 the Penns still retained large tracks of land and sold the privilege of mining coal in the great seam to any one who would pay thirty pounds for a coal lot. Thus, the coal trade was started in South Western Pennsylvania. In 1860 the Westmoreland Coal Co. opened a mine west of Manor. Twenty five years later, the Jim-Town mine was opened. It was then closed about 1917.

For nineteen years after the coal mines had been opened west of Manor, there were very few inhabitants on the site of the present day Manor. Manor was divided North and South by the two tracks of the Pennsylvania Railroad. On the South Side of the tracks was the station building, but it had been moved twice; first, eastward, and second, northward. Joseph McCartney was the first ticket agent. He and his family, three sons and one daughter, wife and maiden sister, Susan, resided in the west end of the station. Aunt Susan McCartney had the first Christmas tree in Manor.

Next to the station grounds were the stock yards. From this point car after car was loaded with cattle, sheep, and hogs for shipment. Located beside the stockyards was Miller's grain depot which is the present borough building. Car after car was loaded with wheat, oats, and corn to be shipped from the depot. Mr. Miller, who was Dr. A. D. Miller's father, paid cash for the grain which had a tendency to increase his business.

On the upper side of the mill, Mrs. Walthour lived with her three sons and three daughters. On the back of the lot was the livery stable which was later moved. Next to the Walthour property was one of Manor's first hotels owned by Mrs. Heintzelman; at the extreme end of the street was Isaac Baer's lumber mill; this was Manor's leading industry at that time. The rest of the street was very much the same as it is today except for a few additions and changes.

Near Isaac Baer's lumber mill and at the site of the present culvert was the start of the old mill race. The mill race followed the course of the present day Jeannette-Manor road and then ran parallel with Race Street, going under the railroad tracks from south side to north side and to its objective, the Kifer mill which was later known as the Altman mill.

All places built along the mill race on the south side of Manor had to be approached by plank crossings over the mill race. The total number of buildings both commercial and private homes was thirty-two on the south side of the railroad.

Most of the north side of the railroad was taken up by Painter's farm and large orchard. Later, the Ludwick Estate was purchased from the Kifers at a Sheriff's sale in 1879. A farm house which was later sold to David Caldwell in 1914 and this home is now owned by Margaret Brennan who at the present time resides in this home. The old spring house was located on the former Dr. Shirey's ground which is the present Manor Post Office Building and parking lot. What is now the United Church of Christ is where the barn stood. There were very few houses on the north side except those that were built along Railroad Street and Race Street.

Mr. Ludwick, after purchasing the farm began a sale of lots known as the "Orchard Plan." Most of the lots sold for between one hundred and two hundred dollars. After the town of Manor had been layed out under the "Orchard Plan," it was incorporated into a borough in 1890.

Manor Borough continued to grow on the strength of its pioneer industries and the addition of later commercial units. With the increase of population came the need for a school, churches, a bank, a government, post office, and places of entertainment.

Manor had four school houses. The first was built on the property at the juncture of Brush Creek and Bushy Run Creek at the south eastern corner, this location was occupied by the Freedom Oil Company in later years. The next school house was built in the middle of the 19th century; it consisted of two rooms and was a two story building. The building was kept propped up by telephone poles. This school house was torn down and the lumber sold to Mr. Grable. The two story building was replaced by a three roomed school. While this school was being built, school was held in Dr. Griffith's stable, which is now the house on the back of what was Dr. Snyder's lot, presently this lot is the Joseph Crock property. Manor's present school was built in the early part of the 20th century.

Since there were no churches in Manor, the first school building was used for both a school and a church. The first school building was one room, which contained three stumps for seats and one pot bellied stove. During the middle of the 19th century another school was constructed on a hillside, at that time the lot was located in the "Orchard Plan;" and today in 1976, the location is the corner of Broadway Street and Blaine Avenue.

The first church to be established was the Methodist Church in 1872. Several years after this the Presbyterian Church was built in the midst of Painter's orchard. In the year of 1885, the old Painter barn was torn down; the foundation stone reset and upon this new foundation was built the Reformed Church. The Lutheran Church was constructed in 1902.

The first post office was located where now stands O'Bryan's store. This was established in the middle of the 19th century. Mr. Jim McWilliams was the first Post Master. When President Cleveland came into office, the Republican Post Master was replaced by Mr. Brinker. Later, the post office was moved to Wilson's building, now occupied by a furniture upholsterer. This building is located next to the present day newstand. Then the post office was moved in the Manor National Bank building. When this building was demolished, the post office was temporarily placed in the building where Dvorsky's Costume shop is now located. Later, a new post office was constructed on the present site on Atlantic Avenue.

The Heinzelman Hotel was one of the first in Manor and was located in the old Emerson building, then Smith's place on Railroad Street. The other hotels were the Morrow House, Douglas Hotel, Flarathy's Commercial Hotel, and Hesa's Hotel, then Anthony's building, and at present it is known as the McElfresh building.

Manor's first theater was the Opera House located on the entire second floor of what was known as the Sowash building, presently owned by Mr. Paul Lehman.

Most of Manor's pioneer industries have been discontinued due to changing conditions. Two of the most prominent industries to close were the Pick Handle Factory established in 1861 by Michael Beamer and later operated by Paul Beamer, and the Distillery founded in 1878 by Jacob Mathias and Dominick Fry. Some of the pioneer merchandisers were Mr. Gress, Jack Best, C. C. Hershey, William Beamer, Frank Fry, Jim McWilliams, Mr. Morrow, Mr. Poole, Paul Brinker, Piersons, Hippards, Mrs. Woodrow and H. A. Lauffer. A few of these business locations have been replaced with new businesses.

In 1907, the Manor streets (at that time) were paved, eliminating old board sidewalks and mud thoroughfares. A very important change was the elimination of the Race Street Grade Crossing in 1926 by the Pennsylvania Railroad Company under contract to the J. C. Casey Company.

Present day Manor is not considered an industrial center but more a residential district.

6

GENERAL

FORT WALTHOUR and WALTHOUR MILL

The history of Fort Walthour, the Walthour grist mill and other buildings was compiled by Frank Probst Walthour in the year 1920. In this same year he prepared a scroll of the Walthour Family Tree and carried it out to the 7th generation. There are about 409 names on this scroll plus the outline of the mill, log house, barn and other utility buildings. By these records the Walthour brothers, Christopher Conrad and George Jacob had left Holland about 1750 and landed in Georgia. Before landing, they were overtaken by the Spaniards; who at this time had great influence along the coast of Georgia and Florida.

Picture courtesy - Ethel King

GENERAL VIEW OF THE WALTHOUR FARM

A view of the Walthour grist mill taken from the direction of Westmoreland City.

This steel bridge over Brush Creek, replaced an old wooden bridge which was probably built by the settlers themselves.

The road running past the front of the mill intersected another road, which today is known as Sandy Hill road.

On the near side of the grist mill is a utility building, and in the center rear is the red brick Walthour home.

They had carried a wooden-backed Bible with them from Holland and at this point the Bible was tossed into the water. The Walthour's were set free by the Spaniards and they recovered the Bible. They did not become established in Georgia but moved north along the Atlantic Coast, and finally settled in Berks County, Pennsylvania. Later, the settlers started to move west across the Alleghenies securing and establishing claims in this region.

The Walthours were among the first settlers and they secured a claim next to Adam Radebaugh. The reported claim was said to be 906 acres but later found to be 1,060 acres.

This same Bible was used in Fort Walthour and many years later was placed in a glass case in the auditorium of the "ZION LUTHERAN CHURCH," Greensburg, Pennsylvania.

Walthour Mill

A grist mill, a saw mill, a log cabin, utility shed, and a barn were built. This grist mill according to Frank Probst Walthour's records, was built about 1758. The location was near by the confluence of Brush Creek and Bushy Run Creek.

Picture courtesy - Mrs. Homer Naley

WALTHOUR GRIST MILL AND LOG HOUSE

The grist mill was one of the first buildings built in this immediate vicinity.

8

Not long after the settlers moved in, a church was organized about 3 miles east of Fort Walthour and was attended by most of these settlers.

The Brush Creek Church was organized about 1773.

The settlers grew most of the grain for the grist mill, but salt, tools, hardware, and other supplies had to be secured from the east. The grist mill was run by water power, as a dam had been built on Brush Creek at a location close to the present railroad culvert at the eastern end of South Railroad Street and a mill race led away from the dam and followed a course similar to the flow of Brush Creek.

When homes were built in this location later, part of the mill race was covered with boards.

A street laid out many years later followed a course similar to the mill race itself, the origin of the street's name, "Race Street" then remains the same name today.

Later, following the building of the grist mill, a brick home was built across the road from the mill, in about the year 1783; and still later a wing was added to the back of the home.

Picture courtesy - Mabel Caldwell

CLOSE-UP VIEW OF WALTHOUR GRIST MILL

9

Levi Paul Naley, born on his father's farm on Jan. 17, 1819, in Penn Township, worked on the farm till his marriage, and later worked in this Walthour grist mill.

Frank Wilkins, who was living in the red brick home of the Walthours in 1915, recovered enough lumber out of the grist mill to build a cabin on the hillside above the grist mill.

The brick home had always been occupied, and today in 1976 the Charles Davis family occupies the home.

There was no record of when the mill ceased operations but these buildings were built about the Revolutionary War days and were still standing until the year 1915; when they were dismantled.

At the time of dismantling, one of the circular stones for the grinding of the grain was removed from the mill and placed on the Mathias property, later to become the Howard Whitehead property.

Many of the children of Manor played in these old buildings in the early 1900's; little did they realize they were playing in buildings built before the American Revolution.

Fort Walthour

After the grist mill was built, a fort, stockade, or block house was built at a point 3 miles south of the grist mill about 1774. The fort was used by the settlers in this vicinity as a place of defense, retreat, or a place to live during Indian attacks and forays of which there were many. Many tales have been told about the kidnappings, the scalpings and plundering in the immediate vicinity.

Picture courtesy - Mrs. Homer Naley

STEEL BRIDGE TO WALTHOUR GRIST MILL

10

In the middle 1900's a plaque was placed on old Route 30, beside what was then the Michael Clohessy Farm, and near the Irwin Terminal of the Pennsylvania Turnpike; just a short distance east from the present-day Murphy Mart on Route 30, to identify the location of the old Fort Walthour.

Picture corutesty - Mabel Caldwell

WALTHOUR MILL AND BLACKSMITH SHOP

This view of the Walthour grist mill shows the wooden bridge over Brush Creek; black building at left was the blacksmith shop.

A log cabin was next to the grist mill with the large barn and utility building at the left.

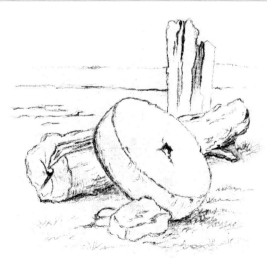

Illustration courtesy - Emily Munson Shirey

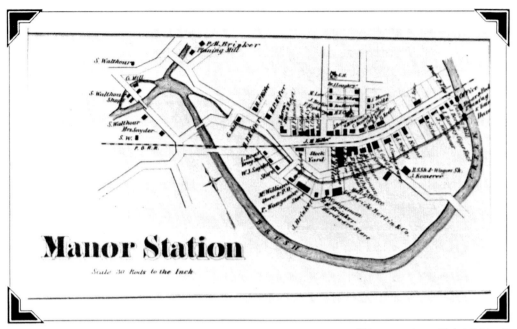

Manor Station

Scale 30 Rods to the Inch

PICTORIAL VIEW OF MANOR STATION

The railroad was in the center of this view from left to right; the stock yard was in the center of this view.

Most of the business places were located on the south side of the railroad, and most of the residences were on the north side of the railroad.

The course of the mill race shown here started at a dam on Brush Creek near the planing mill of Baer and Pool, followed a course on the south side of the railroad, thence to the north side of the railroad to a mill which was operated by Mr. Painter, H. P. Kifer, Jim McWilliams, and last by Hiram Altman.

The mill race continued to the confluence of Brush Creek and Bushy Run Creek, where a dam serviced the Walthour mill.

THE BERT EATON LOG HOME ON SANDY HILL ROAD

This log home on Sandy Hill Road is still standing today in 1976, was purchased in 1922 as a residence by Bert Eaton, from the McCutcheon heirs of Pittsburgh. The McCutcheon family never lived in this home, they only secured this property to sell the coal rights to the Westmoreland Coal Co. operating nearby.

At the time of purchase of this log home by Mr. Eaton, it was said that the age of the property was over 150 years. The Eaton family made an attempt to trace back to the first deed, but it was probably burned at the Hannastown Courthouse.

This log home on Sandy Hill Road was 1/2 mile north of the location of the old Walthour Grist Mill located at the confluence of Brush Creek and Bushy Run Creek.

The Walthour Grist Mill, and the Eaton Log Home, both well over 200 years old, were probably the first buildings ever erected in the immediate Manor vicinity.

Rose bushes were in evidence around the back porch in this picture, but the large rose bush to the right of the porch was a rose of a bright blue color, which was a rarity in this vicinity at this period of time.

W. Eaton had hauled bricks by team and sand from the Sandy Hill Road location for the paving of Manor Borough Streets in the year 1907.

MICHAEL BEAMER

This picture is of Michael Beamer, founder, owner and operator of the M. Beamer and Son Handle Manufacturers.

Michael Beamer's son William also operated a drug store on Race Street.

FRONT VIEW M. BEAMER & SON
HANDLE MANUFACTURERS

This early plant of the Beamer Handle Co., was built by Michael Beamer in 1861. They supplied pick handles to the coal mining industry, also shipped axe handles, hammer handles and hatchet handles, all over the Eastern United States.

This location was on Brush Creek, in back of the present Manor American Legion Home.

END VIEW M. BEAMER HANDLE COMPANY

The large store in center rear was built by H. A. Lauffer, later run by J. R. Sowash and today is occupied by Lehman's Manor Market.

The large earth fill in the center, plus the trestle formed the roadbed for the Manor Valley Railroad. A small station and rail platform were located in back of the handle plant.

The dirt road in center foreground crossed Brush Creek and under the railroad trestle, then ran past the H. A. Lauffer store to Race Street.

This home is now owned by Chuck Charrie

FORMER BEAMER HOME 2005

BEAMER HANDLE COMPANY

This large modern handle factory was built in 1903 to replace the old Beamer Handle Company.

This plant employed about 50 to 60 men, and they, too produced pick handles, hatchet handles, axe handles and hammer handles that were shipped all over Eastern United States.

The crossing at the left and the road that led away from it, ran past the front of the plant, crossed Brush Creek and continued past the Walthour farm and out the Sandy Hill road.

At right center are large oil storage tanks, owned by Freedom Oil Company, whose oil depot was located at the bridge over Bushy Run Creek. M. B. Walker was manager of this Freedom Oil Depot. In 1910 this plant burned to the ground and was rebuilt by the Nassua Steel Company. In early 1919 this factory burned again. H and H Foundries occupies this site today, utilizing the remains of the building.

The Beamer Handle Company later moved to the top of Hill Street where it was operated by Paul Beamer, grandson of Michael Beamer.

BEAMER HANDLE COMPANY
A VIEW OF THE BEAMER HANDLE CO., AFTER IT WAS
DESTROYED BY FIRE IN 1910

16

H. A. LAUFFER STORE – NORTH RACE STREET

H. A. Lauffer, born on a farm between Harrison City and Claridge in March 1850, worked on the farm until maturity and then opened a store in Penn Station in 1876. He later moved to Irwin and opened a shoe store there in 1883. Later he moved to Manor and built this mammoth store in 1886.

The store stocked dry goods, groceries, carpets, furniture, hardware and shoes.

This building had apartments, and a large auditorium on the second floor which was the scene of Saturday night dances, plays and a decade or more of basketball. "Uncle Tom's Cabin" once played in this auditorium.

On the first floor was a series of storerooms, a doctor's office, a harness shop run by Mr. Issett, a Chinese laundry run by Ho Sang, later by Sam Sang, and on the far end of the building was the office of the Justice of the Peace, Mr. P. H. Naley.

H. A. Lauffer, besides operating this large store, was elected as a Director of the First National Bank of Irwin, when it was organized in 1893, and was elected the first President of Manor National Bank when it was organized in 1902.

This location is now the Manor Market.

P. R. BRINKER AND SON
FARM IMPLEMENT DISPLAY

Picture courtesy - Martin Dvorsky

P. R. Brinker and Son, agents for Deering Farm Implements and Machinery, and Superior Farm Implements and Supplies, had a large display here which was attended by a large crowd of local farmers, some from the Denmark Manor District.

P. R. Brinker had a large store on Race Street which is now the location of O'Bryan's appliances. In the rear of this store was a large warehouse with storage space for hardware and farm supplies.

In the center of this picture is the old Town Hall, with a fire bell hanging in the tower. The date of construction of the old Town Hall is not available, but it probably was built about the same time that the Borough of Manor was incorporated, which was on January 4, 1890. Hidden in back of the Town Hall was the jail, a small building containing two steel cells. Frequent occupants of this jail were transients who were seeking a night's lodging.

The white building on the left, owned by Mr. Miller, was used as a grainery and feed supply house. Later this building was acquired by Mr. Miller's son, Dr. A. D. Miller. It was later acquired by Manor Borough, and is now the Manor Borough Building.

The fence and stockade in view in front of the grainery were used to contain cattle, which were driven here from surrounding farms and nearby counties. A ramp led from the stockade to cattle cars on the siding of the Pennsylvania Railroad. From here the cattle were shipped to the eastern market.

The large I.O.O.F. building to the right of the Town Hall was the meeting place of several lodges. Dances were also held in this hall. This Odd

Fellows Hall was destroyed by fire February 2, 1911, and was later replaced by a building erected by the Manor Rod and Gun Club.

The Rod and Gun Club building was later gutted by fire, but was rebuilt and outfitted with a social room, bowling alleys, and pool room.

Later, the front of this building was used for barber shops which were operated at different times by Jack Caldwell and George Higgins.

In more recent years, this building was acquired by Paul Franklin, and was used as a tin and furnace shop. This furnace shop was then acquired by Franklin's sons and Mr. Brown.

The building to the left of the I.O.O.F. Hall was the livery stable built by Rush Walthour, and later run by his son, Spike Walthour. This livery was still in business in the first quarter of the 1900's. To the left was another livery stable, owned and managed by the McElfresh family.

The flag in the center of this picture contained 44 stars, the flag of 1890.

You can also see dirt streets, a buggy parked on the sidewalk, and a covered wagon parked in front of the I.O.O.F. Hall.

Lighting poles shown here were installed in 1893, and lines were strung that same year.

*   Manor Electric Co. was organized and chartered in April 1892 by the Beamer Family. This power plant was built and went into service in 1893.

*   The Manor Electric Co. plant contained one of the larger dynamos built at the Garrison Alley plant of George Westinghouse. This same dynamo was on exhibition at the Chicago World's Fair Columbian Exposition in 1893, and came to Manor the same year. The dynamo was the alternating current type, a development of George Westinghouse himself.

*   Used with the Westinghouse dynamo was a 'secondary converter', later to be know as a transformer.

*   (Notes from George Westinghouse Life History)

A DESTRUCTIVE BLAZE

The Business Portion of Manor Goes Up in Smoke. An Entire Block Burned, Aggregating a Loss of $35,000 - - - Eleven Families Homeless - - - Insurance Light.

Manor Station, about three miles west of Jeannette, was visited at an early hour Wednesday morning by one of the most destructive fires ever witnessed in this vicinity. The fire was discovered about 5 o'clock, and started in the rear of Painter's bakery and confectionery store, on Race Street, and had gained such headway that all efforts to extinquish it proved futile. Some, of the occupants barely escaped with their lives in their night clothes. The alarm soon brought out almost the entire population of the town, but with their poor facilities for fighting fire, they were unable to do but little towards checking the progress of the flames, which soon spread to adjoining buildings on either side. A telegram was sent to Pittsburgh for help, and the generous response was received that if the citizens of the town would guarantee $500, they would send an engine out. Irwin was then appealed to. The sturdy citizens of that place grasped the situation, and calling her fire department together and procuring a special train, were soon on their way to the scene of the conflagration. By this time the fire had destroyed the bakery, the Ludwick building on the north, Beamer's residence, Snyder's Hotel, Rankin and Brinker's storeroom, P. R. Brinker's large storeroom and dwelling, and was fast devouring the large Waugaman building on the south. The first company lost no time after their arrival, and soon had the fire under control. Had it not been for their timely arrival the residence of the widow Brinker would certainly have been destroyed and probably several others. The buildings destroyed were all frame, dry, and burned rapidly. It is thought the loss will reach about $35,000, with but small insurance. Quite a number of the victims lost all they had. The origin of the fire is still a mystery.

(The article went on to list the names of the tenants, estimated loss, and insurance coverage.)

The Manor Valley News - Volume I - No. 1 - Devoted to the interests of Manor Valley.
Manor Station, Pa., Thursday, December 4, 1890
Jas. R. Orr, Publisher
$1.00 per year in advance

From the Scrapbook of Michael Beamer - No date given on clippings
Contributed by Mrs. Henry R. Patterson

J. MATHIAS AND CO. DISTILLERY

The Mathias distillery was founded in the late 1800's, and was operated by the same family for many years.

Their major product was Manor Pure Rye Whiskey.

Later, Mr. Fry became a partner in the business which existed until the passing of the 18th Amendment.

When the Manor National Bank was organized, Mr. Joseph Mathias became the first Vice President.

The location was at the beginning of the Brush Creek Road.

FRY AND MATHIAS DISTILLERY

Fry and Mathias organized a distillery operation in the year 1878.

A pig pen was included in this operation, because they fed the mash to the pigs. The first distillery burned down, but it was replaced immediately in 1882 with a large new distillery, bond house, and other utility buildings.

At the left is the red frame distillery; at the right, the concrete block building which was the bond house, and in the front are other utility buildings.

J. MATHIAS AND CO. BONDED WAREHOUSE

The bonded warehouse of J. Mathias and Co, was adjacent to the distillery.

The warehouse, built at a cost of $12,000.00 had a capacity of 3,000 barrels. The old warehouse had a capacity of 1,500 barrels. Both were located on the Brush Creek road.

Their advertising guaranteed prompt delivery of all orders received by phone or mail.

THE DOUGLASS HOTEL

The Douglass Hotel was located on South Race Street, near the railroad and handy to the rail depot. The hotel advertised 22 neatly furnished rooms, ample baths, and a well appointed office.

This hotel business was established by Mr. Alexander Pool in 1890, and later taken over by Mr. Douglass.

The hotel was later operated by Charley Maher, and then by the McWilliams family.

The hotel was completely dismantled when subways for automobiles and pedestrians were constructed.

22

CANDLELIGHT TO ELECTRIC LIGHT

Mature citizens of Manor in the year 1900, would have lived through a period of time in which there were great changes to them, comparable to the great changes witnessed by citizens living through 76 years of the 20th century.

In 1830-1840, candlelight, whale oil light, and olive oil light, were the sources of lighting.

Wood was the source of fuel, but outcroppings of coal were all over Westmoreland County.

Transportation was by horse, horse and buggy, or walking.

Agriculture was the general occupation, as all the hardware and household supplies came from the Eastern Seaboard.

Water supplies came from springs, dug wells or hand pumping wells and there were no sanitary facilities, either inside the homes or outside the house.

Fire was known to all generations; even the ancient Egyptians knew how to use and make fire. In ancient Persia, which is now Iran, one of the largest oil producing nations in the world, there were large seepages of oil, and they had large permanent fires burning. Around these, the fire worshippers built altars and conducted their religious services.

The Eastern Seaboard having been developed, the railroads were put through to Pittsburgh, which started an industrial period.

Coal mines were opened on spur branch lines of the Pennsylvania Railroad around 1860, which gave employment to many citizens in Westmoreland County. An iron works had opened in downtown Pittsburgh, which furnished a large supply of cannon and shells to the North during the Civil War.

Other small industries were opened, and with the drilling and discovery of gas at Murrysville about 1878, methods were developed to handle the gas and pipe it into the towns.

Some of the towns had gas lights on the streets, which consisted of upright pipes with the gas burning at the end.

Later, gas was piped into some homes. With a special cloth mantle and valve, gas light was put to use in the homes. Gas was also used for cooking in the cast iron stoves which were the main source of heat.

The coming of gas meant the opening of many glass factories.

One of the first great industrialists to come on the scene in Pittsburgh was George Westinghouse.

He was born in Central Bridge, New York in 1846, moved to Schenectady in 1856, and later studied math and engineering at Union College.

He served in the Civil War first as a cavalryman, then later as a naval engineer.

George and his father, who was a man of wealth, came to Pittsburgh in 1867, and became involved in industrial work at once. George heard of the boring of the tunnel under the Alps in Switzerland, the Mount Cenis Tunnel, and made a trip over there. Seeing how they were boring this tunnel, with compressed air tools, he came back to Pittsburgh and decided to put that idea to work.

George Westinghouse and Ralph Baggely built and perfected the air brake for the railroads, and in 1868 it was first tried on the Panhandle Railroad.

It proved a success and later, the legislators in the eastern states passed legislation requiring the railroads to install air brakes.

George Westinghouse, in 1869, organized Westinghouse Air Brake Co. which began supplying air brakes to the railroads of the United States.

Later, the giant plant was built at Wilmerding, Pa. to serve the railroad industry.

George Westinghouse was president of this air brake plant until his death in 1914.

After developing the air brake, he did not stop there, as he was known as a man of many ideas.

In 1871, George Westinghouse bought a large mansion on Lang Avenue in Homewood, and had a large workshop on the premises.

While living in this mansion, he drilled a gas well in his back yard in 1884.

On May 21, 1884 the drilling foreman notified George Westinghouse that they were hitting small pockets of gas, so they kept on drilling.

At 3 A.M. the next morning, there was a continuous explosion; George Westinghouse looked out the window and saw that the derrick was flattened and nobody was in sight. A giant bath of mud and water had covered everything, including George's prize Ginkgo trees.

After the initial roar died down, pure gas came from the drilling hole, and within a week, George and his partners developed an apparatus which was able to shut off the flow and regulate it.

George Westinghouse's neighbors were scared of this project and they called it the Pit of Damnation.

Other wells were drilled later, and in conjunction with the Murrysville wells, gas was piped under the Pittsburgh streets. This was the beginning of what was later known as the Equitable Gas Co.

But, George did not stop here. He heard about a Frenchman named Lucien Gaulard, and an Englishman by the name of John Dixon Gibbs who were experimenting with alternating current and its distribution. So, George made a trip to France to observe on the spot, this newfangled idea. He returned to Pittsburgh where he and some of his engineers soon developed their own version of alternating current.

Westinghouse and his group secured a building at Garrison Alley and Fayette Street in downtown Pittsburgh, next to the Allegheny River.

It was here they developed the alternating current dynamo used with a secondary converter.

Edison had just developed the first incandescent light bulb, which was used with direct current. The eastern interests were backing Edison, and the Pittsburgh interests were backing Westinghouse. This was known as the battle of the currents.

Edison wrote, "My personal opinion would be to prohibit entirely, the use of alternating currents", classing it as dangerous.

Westinghouse went on to perfect this alternating current dynamo, and secure the patent rights.

But during this battle of the currents, a financial strain was put on the Pittsburgh group, and Westinghouse, known by every man working for him, had the loyalty of the whole group.

One of the group who was the first to be associated with Westinghouse, was a long-time resident of Manor, Jimmie Steiner, of Observatory Street.

By Jimmie Steiner's account, Westinghouse came through the plant during this financial pinch, called all the employes together, and asked them to forego part of their wages, which they did.

Later, he secured land in East Pittsburgh and Trafford.

Jimmie Steiner served for many years as General Foreman in the E aisle at the giant East Pittsburgh Plant.

George Westinghouse secured the contract to light the Chicago Worlds Fair Columbian Exposition in 1893, which proved very successful. At this Worlds Fair, he had on exhibition some of his alternating current dynamos and other electrical equipment.

After the end of the Worlds Fair, electrical equipment was being secured by some communities, and one of the larger Westinghouse dynamos on exhibition at the Fair came to Manor.

The Beamer family was the primary organizer of the Manor Electric Co., and it was chartered in April 1892.

They purchased land from the Penn Gas Coal Company and built a plant, in which was installed the dynamo from the Worlds Fair.

This dynamo was of a large capacity, and was able to supply Jeannette, Penn, Manor, and Irwin with power.

Poles were set up in Manor in 1893 and later the lines were strung.

People going from candlelight to kerosene light, to gas light, and now to electric light was said to be like coming out of the Dark Ages.

At this time 'Jubilation' was the term of the day. As one prominent citizen in Jeannette remarked, we now have a fully rounded program. We have a Church, we have a School, we have a Newspaper, we have a Lighting Company, and we have a Saloon.

The Church represents - Sanctification.
The School represents - Education.
The Newspaper represents - Publication.
The Light Company represents - Illumination.
The Saloon represents - Damnation.

The development of alternating current started the fast industrialization of the United States. Seventy-six years of changes like the auto, airplane, radio, telephone, television, atomic bomb, missiles, trips to the moon, medical developments, and thousands of others followed.

George Westinghouse died on March 12, 1914 in New York City.

The Westinghouse Corporation furnished employment to more Manor citizens than any other industry in this location.

(Westinghouse data taken from life history of George Westinghouse)

WALTHOUR LIVERY STABLE

This stable was established by Benjamin Rush Walthour in August 1876, and was successfully operated by him until his death in 1903, when his son Howard Cherry Walthour took over the business. The livery could accommodate 30 horses, and had 16 head, along with 12 buggies, 3 runabouts and 6 carriages for hire.

Later, the business was operated by Kistler and Sowash; but with the coming of the automobile, the livery business came to a halt.

On the left of this view, was another livery conducted by Nevin McElfresh.

The location of these livery stables was directly across South Race Street from the Manor Borough Building.

LUDWICK HOME

Originally this home was the residence of the H. P. Kifer farm, which Ludwick had purchased from H. P. Kifer.

The barn stood on the corner, which is now the location of the Manor United Church of Christ.

Mr. Ludwick laid out the Orchard Plan of lots in 1879, which included the hill up from Race Street.

The Ludwick estate was settled in 1914 and this home was purchased by David H. Caldwell.

DOG NEEDS A DRINK

This watering trough was located on Brush Creek Road near the bridge and next to the old "Fry and Mathias" distillery.

ALTMAN MILL

About 1896, Hiram Altman and Minerva Shader Altman with their two children, R. Stacey and Gertrude, moved to Manor to the home adjacent to the home of Homer Naley on Observatory Street. Clair Altman was born in this house.

Hiram Altman and his brother-in-law, Martin Goehring of West Newton, opened a general store located on Race Street, at the corner which is now across the street from O'Brien's Appliance store, and adjacent to the hotel. A movie house later occupied this property. Later, Hiram Altman bought the feed mill from Mr. J. M. McWilliams. Mr. Altman and his sons operated this mill for many years.

The location of this mill was on the corner lot which is presently occupied by the Manor American Legion building. After the mill was torn down, the Altmans donated the ground for the Manor Legion Home.

Altman's mill was moved to Irwin and an additional mill was acquired in Troy, Ohio. From this small mill in Manor this business made great progress in Irwin and in Troy. At one point, forty trucks were employed to carry on daily operations.

With the passing of the older members of the family, this milling business came to a halt.

H. Clair Altman is the last surviving member of this family. He is 78 years old and resides with his wife, Doll Simpson Altman, on their farm near Strawpump.

H. Clair Altman and Doll S. Altman

TAYLOR HOUSE

The Taylor home on North Railroad Street was at the corner of Cleveland Avenue.

This home was occupied in the late 1800's by Mrs. Rachael Caldwell.

ANTIQUE CAR

This antique car—make, model or year not identified—has right hand steering and chain drive. Manorites out for a spin are, (left to right), Franklin Fry and Homer Naley.

HORSE AND BUGGY AT THE J. R. SOWASH STORE

Horses and buggies parked in front of the J. R. Sowash store in Shafton. There were no gas woes with this type of traveling. Seated in the buggy in this view are Franklin Fry (left) and Homer Naley (right). Must be school days; some of the children on the left are holding books in their arms. The little girls at the rear wore fancy hats to school. The location of this picture was the road leading to the bridge, which crossed the main line of the Pennsylvania Railroad at Shafton Station. Two sets of steps led from the bridge down to the station platforms. The top sign on the store here reads, "Sherwin-Williams Paints", and directly under this sign, the owner and operator of the store at this time, Mr. J. R. Sowash. J. R. Sowash secured this store property from Mr. McKeever in the year 1898. This was the beginning of many decades of store business by the Sowash Family. J. R. Sowash's younger brother, J. K. Sowash, later operated a general store on Ligonier Street in Latrobe.

J. R. Sowash continued operation of the Shafton store until about the year 1905, at which time he became involved in a land deal in the western states. His younger brother, J. K. Sowash, took over the operation of the Shafton store at this time. J. R. Sowash and his wife left on this trip to the western states. They settled in the state of Idaho where their first child, Sarah, was born. After completing this western mission, they returned to the town of Manor in 1907. J. R. Sowash immediately secured and took over the operation of the giant H. A. Lauffer store in this same year. They secured a residence directly across the street from the store, later known as the Kemerer home.

Later, J. R. Sowash secured a home on Hill Street which they occupied for a short period of time. Finally securing a residence on Observatory Street, they established a permanent home at this location.

The Lauffer Store, later the Sowash Store, was occupied by a large variety of tenants during the years. There was an auditorium on the second floor, used for dancing, plays, and basketball. The establishments housed here included Dr. C. Snyder, Sr.; a butcher shop business established by the Lomicka Brothers, Jim and Andy; a harness repair shop by Mr. Isett; a Chinese laundry business run by Ho Sang, later by Sam Sang; several plumbing businesses, one run by a Mr. Porter; apartments on the second floor and Justices of the Peace, P. H. Naley and Mr. Holden. The store business in the early 1900's was on a large scale and a team drawn delivery was in operation at this time to outlying communities: Harrison City, Pleasant Valley and Clark's Crossing.

A long list of personnel worked at this store at one time or another: J. W. Smeltzer, H. Myers, Chal. Kistler, J. McWilliams, John Stubbs, Jim Fink, Agnes Fenwick, Miss Grace and others.

Later the Sowash family took over complete operation of this store on Race Street. At the time of the wagon delivery, a barn was used to store wagons and stable the horses. This location was at Creek Side which is now the location of the Legion's lower parking lot. With the advent of the automobile and trucks, horse and wagon delivery was discontinued and a truck was secured for delivery. Jim Fink was the horse and wagon delivery driver, and later the truck driver.

Picture courtesy - Mrs. Homer Naley
Store data courtesy of Helen Sowash

Picture courtesy - Elsie Lauffer

STONE SPRINGHOUSE

This stone springhouse was on the residential property of
Dr. C. A. Shirey, now occupied by the Manor Post Office.
Springhouses and block ice coolers were very prominent
before the age of the electric refrigerator.

THE SOWASH FAMILY AND STORE HISTORY

OBSERVATORY STREET HOME 1909

John R. Sowash was born in 1874 and raised on a farm in Claridge, PA. In 1898 he owned and operated a store in Shafton when he became involved in a land deal out West. He married Emma B. Whiteman who was born in Gratztown in 1883. They left in 1905 for Weiser, Idaho. Their first-born child, Sara, arrived on November 26, 1906. They returned to Manor in 1907 and took over the operation of the giant H. A. Lauffer store on Race Street. Later they rented a house directly across the street from the store, which was to be known as the Kemerer home. John, nicknamed Bud, was born on May 14, 1908. In 1909 they purchased a large home on Observatory Street where ten more children were born.

THE SOWASH BUILDING, A MANOR LANDMARK

The store was a large operation and employed many people. There were three huge storerooms. Some of the employees were: J. W. Smeltzer, Henry Myers, Chal Kistler, J. McWilliams, John Stubbs, Howard DeWalt, Agnes Fennwick, Miss Grace, and Mace Detwiler.

GROCERY DEPARTMENT

The store contained a large grocery section as well as a Hardware Department and a Furniture Department. If Sowash didn't have something for you, he'd order it. With customers from Harrison City, McCullough, Claridge, Pleasant Valley and Westmoreland City, he would take orders by telephone then deliver them the next day. He also hauled coal and moved people's belongings.

DRY GOODS DEPARTMENT

In the Sowash Building there were many other businesses: a shoe repair shop, Chinese laundry, roofing and tinning business, Dr. Snyder, Sr., a plumbing shop, Peoples Gas office, and the offices of Justices of the Peace, P. H. Naley and later, Squire Vincent J. Holden.

On the second floor was a large auditorium that was used for dances, plays and basketball. The balance of the second floor contained several apartments.

In 1948 John R. Sowash retired, and the four oldest sons took over the business. They operated in the same way, but remodeled the storefront and made some improvements. They renamed the business "Sowash Brothers." Mick and Ed ran the business after two of the brothers left. They retired in 1968.

All 12 of the Sowash children were reared in Manor, attended Manor School, and the Manor Presbyterian Church. In 1941, four brothers were in the service. Two of the brothers were in the Army and two were in the Marines. Another brother entered the service in 1943, making five Sowash men participants in World War II.

EMMA SOWASH

Helen Sowash was born in 1915. She was married to Charles "Scats" Sundry who died on February 11, 1952. On March 7, 1952, three weeks after the death of her husband, Helen's mother, Emma Whiteman Sowash died. After the death of her father in 1957, Helen moved into the homestead at 39 Observatory Street where she kept house for her four brothers and two sons. She later married Bill Recknor. In 1966, Helen sold the homestead to the present owner, Harry Walter.

OBSERVATORY STREET HOME 2005
OWNED BY HARRY WALTER

Helen states, "I love Manor. It's a close community of people who are not just neighbors, but great friends."

By Helen Sowash

Helen has been an invaluable source of historical facts related to Manor history. She is 90 years old, and is a vibrant and enthusiastic historian, carrying in her head dates of marriages, births, relevant occurrences, and remembrances of things past. She has been an active member of the Book Committee, and her revelations have led to inclusion of facts that may have been lost. Helen lives in Manor on McKelvey Street.

MOVING WILLIAM BEAMER

William Beamer, owner and operator of a drug store on North Race Street, moves from Race Street to Hill Street, which at this period was in Westmoreland City, part of North Huntingdon Township.

There were no moving vans in the late 1800's.

KEMERER MOORE & COMPANY
LUMBER AND PLANING MILL

Checkers is the name of the game.

This view was taken in front of the Kemerer Moore & Company lumber and planing mill, located at the far eastern end of South Railroad Street, next to Brush Creek.

Mr. Baer ran this planing mill in the latter half of the 1800's, Kemerer Moore & Company in the late 1800's and early 1900's, and J. E. Myers in the first quarter of the 1900's.

The mill buildings were dismantled when a new concrete road was constructed and ran thru this location, leading to Wegley, Penn and Jeannette.

Only identified persons in this picture are, Peck Kemerer (far right in the gondola, wearing the topcoat); and sitting on the chair is grey-bearded Mr. Moore.

BOB McCLANAHAN

I. Highberger operated a tin shop on Race Street at approximately the present location of Jay's Barber Shop.

Bob McClanahan was an employee of Highberger and is shown pushing a wheelbarrow containing a roll of tin plate.

The building at the right was Pete Nation's butcher shop.

FRY AND MATHIAS DELIVERY WAGON

A delivery wagon for the Fry and Mathias Distillery Co. is shown on Race Street, in the very early 1900's.

In the driver's seat is Mr. Miller, who lived near the distillery plant.

In the background is the J. P. Wilson property, now the location of Buster Walter's newsstand.

MANOR IN THE EARLY 1900's

This view of Manor shows the Pennsylvania Railroad running right through the center of town. The Manor railroad station is in the center of the picture, and about two hundred feet east is the M.F. control tower, from which all train movements were controlled. In back of the station were interlocking switches.

Nearby is the Miller grainery which is today the location of the Manor Fire Department and the Borough building.

The front of Manor School is shown here, and directly across the street is the red brick Lutheran Church. One block down the hill is the frame structure of the Manor Presbyterian Church, with tower and bell. The Methodist Church is one block east of the Presbyterian Church.

The arrow in the picture points to the home of C. F. Steffy who was involved in one of the big Manor railroad wrecks.

At far right is the overhead bridge which crosses the railroad to Cleveland Avenue.

The lower right corner shows the location of the Harry Steiner Saw and Planing Mill which was powered by a steam engine and was emitting smoke when this picture was taken.

The vacant plot at lower left became well-used tennis courts—until the automobile became popular. This location was then taken over by gasoline filling stations and car repair service stations.

P. H. NALEY

P. H. Naley was Justice of the Peace in Manor in the early 1900's. His office, shown here, was at the north end of the Lauffer store, later the J. R. Sowash store, which today would be in that section of the Manor Market building just recently removed.

All papers, documents, and other legal matters were filed strictly in order, as can be seen in this picture. Any paper, file, or document was at Mr. Naley's fingertips in a matter of a few seconds.

FLAHERTY - COMMERCIAL HOTEL

This hotel, located on South Race Street near the railroad station, was advertised as having 32 nicely furnished rooms with electricity, gas, and fans. These conveniences were also in the barroom. The office and parlor were models of beauty, and the dining room was a model of cleanliness. The room rates were $1.50 per day.

Mr. John L. Flaherty was the owner and proprietor in the early 1900's.

HEASLEY BROTHERS STORE

The Heasley Brothers Store was located at North Railroad Street and Broadway.

Dirt streets were still in existence. The main line of the Pennsylvania Railroad is in the foreground, showing a security fence and a mail post which was used for hanging first class mailbags that were picked up by nonstop mail trains. The mail post and a chute used for receiving mailbags from the trains were later moved west of the Race Street crossing.

Frank E. Heasley (left) and C. R. (Ford) Heasley (holding hand of daughter Bethie), were owners of this store in 1903. George Heasley, another brother, is second from left, and Sam E. Heasley (also a brother) was the driver of the horse drawn delivery wagon.

GENERAL STORE — 1907

A view inside the General Store owned by the Heasley brothers, Ford and Frank in 1907, showed the typical store of early times. This store was located on the corner of North Railroad and Broadway.

These were days of pickle barrels, dried fruit, and crackers and cookies displayed in pasteboard containers.

Electric lights were scarce items at this time. For the most part, gas lights and oil lamps were used for lighting, as can be seen by the two gas lights on the ceiling and the oil lamps for sale on the shelves.

SCHMIDT JEWELRY STORE

S. H. Schmidt operated a jewelry store on South Race Street in the early 1900's. Race Street, at this time, was a dirt road, but a walk was in front of the store for the convenience of pedestrians.

Later, Schmidt moved to East Pittsburgh where he operated a jewelry store on lower Electric Avenue.

HOTEL GRESSLER

The Gressler Hotel was in operation in the late 1800's on Race Street. It had 23 modern, elegantly furnished rooms, a model dining room and kitchen, and a well-stocked bar.

This hotel was later occupied by Frank Beiter, then the Tilbrook family, followed by John Anthony's store and garage.

The location of the hotel was directly across the street from the H. A. Lauffer store, now the Manor Market.

THE JOHN PIERSON STORE

Located on South Race Street in the 1890's, this was a combination food, hardware, and variety store.

It was operated by Mr. and Mrs. Pierson until 1902. Mrs. Pierson is in this picture.

Previously, Pierson operated a store on North Railroad Street in the late 1800's, at the north end of the John Larimer property now owned by Lucinda Sofko.

THE KING STORE

Mr. and Mrs. F. King acquired the Pierson Store on South Railroad Street in 1902. They operated the store for many years.

The King store had a soda fountain and served light lunches. The children loved the penny candy and penny ice cream cones with real ice cream.

Sitting on the stool at the fountain is Chas. Butler.

OAKFORD PARK FLOOD – 1903

Oakford Park, an amusement park in operation during the late 1800's and early 1900's in Jeannette, had a large earthen dam in the valley above the park.

In 1903 the dam, eroded by heavy rains, broke open and a wall of water swept down the tributary that led into Brush Creek. Heavy damage was recorded at all the low lying areas, particularly Jeannette, Penn, and Manor.

Harry Steiner operated a chicken and duck farm in Manor, which is now the property of Oblaks. Most of his buildings, along with the chickens and ducks, were washed downstream to the culvert adjacent to the Pennsylvania Railroad.

LOOKING TOWARD WESTMORELAND CITY

This view was taken looking across the Pennsylvania Railroad from Manor, toward Westmoreland City hill. There were not many houses on the hill at this period of time.

Mr. I. Neleigh, one of the first residents on North Railroad Street in Manor, farmed this hillside in the late 1800's.

WOODEN BRIDGE

This old wooden bridge crossed Brush Creek and led to the Brush Creek road.

In the center of the picture is the location of the present Manor Ball Diamond.

In the rear is a group of buildings including a planing mill, saw mill, storage building, and other utility buildings.

The mill in the center was first operated by Mr. Baier, next by Kemerer-Moore and Co. in the late 1800's, and finally by J. E. Myers.

The mill buildings were removed when a new concrete road was built from Manor to Wegley, and on to Penn and Jeannette.

MANOR VALLEY RAILROAD
ENTERING HARRISON CITY

The people in the center rear of this picture are waiting for the Manor Valley Train.

WHITE STAR LAUNDRY WAGON

Mr. Lawry, manager of the White Star Laundry, established this business in Manor, Westmoreland City, Irwin, and surrounding towns.

Mr. Lawry was an early resident of Manor and lived on South Railroad Street.

This picture was taken in Irwin in the early 1900's, and it shows an Irwin-Herminie traction car.

LOOKING NORTH ON RACE STREET

In this picture, the newsstand is at the left, the Tom Miller building is at the far right, and the old Manor National Bank building is in full view.

The storeroom in the bank, with a canvas awning, was occupied by the Frank Penman Shoe Store.

Picture courtesy - Mrs. Homer Naley

BRUSH CREEK UNION CHURCH REUNION

This annual reunion was an all day affair and was held at the Brush Creek Church in the early 1900's by the Lutheran and Reformed churches. The method of transportation here was horse and buggy. A large refreshment stand can be seen in the center of the activity.

Picture courtesy - Mrs. Homer Naley

DRUGSTORE

Homer Naley and Franklin Fry were partners in this drugstore for a time, but it was operated by Homer Naley himself for many years.

(Left to right), Franklin Fry and Homer V. Naley.

HOMER NALEY'S DRUG STORE

Homer (Skip-a-Dip) Naley owned and operated the only fully equipped drug store in Manor. His nickname, "Skip-a-dip" grew out of his very precise, no surplus servings of Rieck's "Sealtest" ice cream. The several local boys who worked the soda fountain were usually goaded into larger scoops by the various regulars who frequented the Drug Store.

The soda fountain ran along the right wall as you entered the store, with two glass-topped tables on the left for those customers who didn't want to sit at the counter. There was a Bell Telephone booth also along the left wall with a folding door and a light that came on when you closed the door. It was used mostly by young people who wanted to call a friend and have some privacy.

Mr. Naley served customers who came in for the usual drug store items at the back of the store where the then modern electric cash register was located. There was a glass case of cigars along the right wall and the usual brands including the "Marsh Wheeling" stogie. The cash register at the soda fountain was an old mechanical machine that was cranked by hand. Whenever a customer came in to buy a "personal product" of some kind, they would always be served by Mr. Naley instead of a soda boy.

Mr. Naley filled prescriptions exactly as he had learned to do as an apprentice. He still occasionally used the granite "pill forms" to pack the powders he would mix to eventually come out as hardened pills. The drug companies were just beginning to supply prescription pills in bulk quantities.

Some of the regular customers were the two men from the bank across the street. Frank Rankin and Charlie Whitehead would frequently come in at lunch time for snack crackers and milkshakes. Joe Crock who worked at Jim Mellon's funeral home (now Rodgers) was another regular who came for a chocolate milkshake. One of the soda boys, Dick Hauser, accidentally discovered that super cold milk on the verge of freezing would make shakes so thick that the straw wouldn't work. The customers thought it was double ice cream that they were getting. The milkshake business boomed! The most popular fountain drinks were cokes made from two splashes of coke syrup and filled with soda water and ice; ice cream sodas made with chocolate, cherry or pineapple, etc. flavors, vanilla ice cream, and filled with soda water; and the milkshakes.

During WWII. Hershey chocolate bars were scarce, because they were being sent overseas to the troops. Occasionally a box would come in from the supplier. They were doled out very carefully to special customers.

From 1945 on, the soda boys were Bill Hoyer, Dick Hauser, Harold Baughman, Jack Caldwell, and Ronald (Babe) Baughman. In later years the soda fountain was removed.

After Homer's retirement, Mrs. Naley leased the business to druggist Max Applebaum. Two of the local women who worked in the drug store were Ruth Gilchrist and Betty Sproat. The last druggist to own this business was Casper Aleo. The building was empty several years before it was purchased by Howard Walter in 1973. Howard converted the building into two apartments. In 1978 Helen Sowash and Nell Clough were his first two tenants. Mrs. Sisko, the former cook at Manor School, and Helen Sowash live there now.

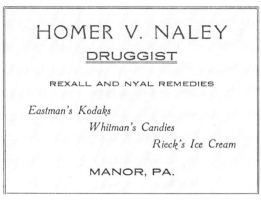

Ad courtesy – 1927 Firemen's Labor Day Program Book

By Dick Hauser

SOME OLD TIME REMEDIES

Fever: Sweet Spirits of Nitre – Use a few drops in warm water with a teaspoon of sugar. No longer available.

Diarrhea: Paregoric – The druggist would usually tell you the amount to use (also in warm water with a little sugar) according to the age and size of the child or adult. It was taken from the market when it was abused by some parents who used it to put their restless children to sleep.

MANOR RAILROAD STATION

This station in the early 1900's consisted of a passenger ticket office, a waiting room, and an express and freight storage and delivery area. It had two sidings, one on each side of the station. A platform extended around three sides of the station, and was at freight car door level, for convenient loading and unloading.

The near side of the station was used mostly for the loading and unloading of freight.

The siding, on the other side of the station, which is under the box car on the extreme left, was used to load and unload heavy freight, on wagons and later on trucks.

A stockade and ramp was to the left, for shipping cattle to the eastern market.

The hand drawn cart shown in the center was used to handle express and mail right from the car doors, as most of the trains were a combination of express, baggage, and mail cars.

The platform at center right crossed all four tracks, and was used to transfer mail and express from westbound to eastbound trains.

Apparatus at center, with short 3-step ladder, was used for outgoing first class mail. There were two steel arms on this pole which could be extended out toward the track.

Outgoing mail was enclosed in a heavy sack with a steel ring on each end.

The station attendant would hang this outgoing mail on the two arms. The mail cars on the train were equipped with a giant hook over one of the mail car doors, and at the approach of the station, this hook was swung out and hooked onto the mail sack without the train slowing down.

Incoming mail was handled in a similar fashion. There were large wooden chutes built close by the tracks and as the train approached the station, mail handlers on the cars tossed the mail sacks out the car doors into these chutes.

The mail trains traveled at a high rate of speed, and these operations had to be carried out with split-second timing.

The coming of the automobile and truck ended this type of operation.

Picture courtesy — Mrs. Ruth Haven

MAIL AND BAGGAGE CART

Two railroad employees from the Manor Station around 1907 were Sam Loughery and Sam Heasley shown with a baggage cart loaded with express boxes ready for pickup.

Picture courtesy - Elsie Lauffer

MANOR CROSSING

This is the crossing on Race Street in 1920 with an unidentified watchman. Mr. J. W. Smeltzer, a Manor merchant is the gentleman wearing the straw hat. The crowd on the platform across the tracks are waiting the arrival of a special picnic train to Idlewild Park.

Picture courtesy - Mrs. Charles Davis

MANOR NATIONAL BANK

The old Manor National Bank on Race Street, which is now the parking lot of the new bank.

The bank was organized in October 1902, and its first officers were President H. A. Lauffer, Vice President Joseph Mathias, Cashier Frank R. Rankin.

The adjoining property, surrounded by the picket fence, was the home of Dr. C. A. Shirey, one of the town's doctors in the early 1900's. This location is now occupied by the Manor Post Office.

INSIDE MANOR NATIONAL BANK CC 1920

Banknote courtesy of Charles D. Whitehead

MANOR NATIONAL BANK NOTE

From 1863 to 1929 the United States government permitted thousands of banks to issue their own notes. They were produced on paper authorized by the government and carried the same basic design. National Bank Notes are still redeemable by the Department of the Treasury at their face value only; however, they may have added value in the numismatic market. This ten dollar note issued by Manor National Bank, dated July 7, 1902, was signed by S. P. Whitehead, President, and Frank R. Rankin, Cashier.

47

MANOR NATIONAL BANK

The three-story brick building was at the northeast corner of Race Street and Atlantic Avenue. The bank and the Frank Penman Shoe Store occupied the first floor. For a while, the U. S. Post Office replaced the shoe store. The dental office of Dr. King, and later on Dr. Adams, and the medical office of Dr. Charles Snyder and Dr. Goff occupied the second floor. The Third floor was used for the functions of various clubs. One of the clubs was the Bachelors' Club, which held dances there.

But the need for growth caused the original bank building to be demolished, and its location became the parking lot for a colonial-style bank building that was completed in 1963. The bank continued to grow. An addition that doubled the size of the new bank was completed in 2001. Architect Jeffrey Schroder, matched the design of the addition to the 1963 bank.

THE NEW BANK

INSIDE MANOR NATIONAL BANK 2005

In 2002, Manor National Bank celebrated its 100th anniversary of banking service to the Manor Community. After the death of President Howard H. Whitehead in 1947, Christ C. Walthour, Jr. served as president of the bank. In an interview by the Tribune Review newspaper, January 30,

2002, Mr. Walthour relates the strength and reliability of Manor Bank during the difficult banking years of the late 1920's and 1930's. He credits the community for this strength. "People in the community actually knew the bank's operators," Walthour said. "Its fiscally conservative policies had earned the trust of the depositors and no bank run occurred."

The growth of business made the need for a bank in Manor at the opening of the 20th Century. "This is a private institution...when a stockholder dies...the shares stay in the family." An example is the Whitehead Family, which was in on the bank's beginnings, and still is actively represented at the bank in 2005. "...Compare that with today's banking practices," Walthour said as he spoke about the bank's financial history. Mr. Walthour was president at the time of his death.

To the present day, the bank is justifiably proud of its ability to have closed only under government orders, and to have re-opened immediately when allowed. It retains the same ideals today.

MANOR BANK BOARD OF DIRECTORS 2002

The advertising hype of the 21st Century has not been needed by Manor National Bank. It retains the small town flavor that its customers prefer. People drive from neighboring communities to bank at this bank that truly knows your name! Yet Manor National Bank has kept pace with the technology used by the larger banks without ever giving up what began in 1902.

The present 2005 officers and directors of the bank are: S. Wayne Whitehead, President, Ross F. Walton, Jr., Vice President, Carl G. Sarge, Cashier and Director, Rand G. Denale, Assistant Cashier and Director. The directors are Renolda B. Whitehead, Walter D. Seigfried, and John F. Rankin.

By S. Wayne Whitehead

1945

1965

NALEY'S BAKERY

Naley's bake shop was in operation in the late 1800's and early 1900's.

This location was at the corner of Race Street and Observatory Street, which is now used as a parking lot for the Manor American Legion.

As shown here, the Naley residence was on the left, and the storeroom was on the right.

In the rear of the storeroom was another building which housed a wagon shed and the bakery itself, including the ovens.

Most of the bakery business was conducted by horse and van delivery wagon, and covered Manor, Harrison City, Pleasant Valley, Clark's Crossing, Claridge and Westmoreland City.

After the dismantling of the bakery, the remaining wagon shed was used as a garage, and the rest of the building housed a shoemaker shop, with apartments on the second floor.

Some of the Naley family resided here after the bakery business was discontinued.

Courtesy - Mrs. Homer Naley

TRANSPORTATION ON RACE STREET

Merchandise and goods were moved by rail, and horse and wagon in the late 1800's. Most railroad stations had express and freight warehouses, where the merchandise was received by rail, and then local delivery was made by horse and wagon. Sitting in the drivers seat here is Emanuel Crum, a resident of Race Street, who is delivering a load of boxes and sacks.

The house in the center is the residence of Dr. C. A. Shirey, which is now the location of the Manor Post Office. The porch post at far left is part of the home of Emanuel Crum, whose property was later acquired and is still owned by Andy Lomicka. It was used as a butcher shop, apartments, and barber shop.

MANOR THEATER

The first motion picture exhibition in town was a nickelodeon around the beginning of the 1900's. It was located next to what was later Franklin's Tin Shop. Within a few years the nickelodeon moved into Burger's Grocery Store and Joe Burger became the operator. This building was on the corner next to the Commercial Hotel.

In 1910-1911 this store was converted into a movie house by building contractor B. M. Yinger. The building was 82 ft. long by 20 ft. wide, and had a center aisle with 90 seats on each side. In the front, a projection booth above and a ticket booth below was installed.

The theater had several owners and operators through the years, one of whom was Frank Echart in 1916 and 1917. The music and sound effects for the silent movies in those days were furnished by piano players Miss Alice Simpson and Howard Schroder.

In 1919 the theater was purchased by Rose Zoppetti, with Squire Naley and Howard Whitehead assisting in the title transfer. Hand cranking the silent films was done by Rose's brother Cherry Zoppetti. Piano players during this time were Thelma Lessig and Ted Blake, who occasionally had a violin accompanist, a relative of the Zoppetti family.

Rose married Mr. Beretta, and their son, Carl, became the manager and custodian, living in the apartment above.

By 1939, the Berettas' sold the theater to the Battison family and their son Wally became the manager.

Charles Harrison was the last person to take over the Manor theater and he kept it operating until the doors finally closed in 1950.

Painting Courtesy – George Y. Heasley

The background music for the silent movies was played on a piano. Slow music represented normal action and fast music represented more forceful action. Piano players included: Alice Simpson, Margaret Lauffer, Howard Schroder, Thelma Lessig, Jane Kooser and Ted Blake. When sound was installed public interest increased. Claridge bus line charted a bus to the movie each week. Occasionally, when the film would be seen melting on screen, the building would shake from booing and stomping of feet.

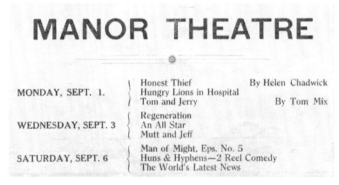

Advertisement courtesy - September 1919 Labor Day Program

MANOR *(THE ELITE)* THEATRE

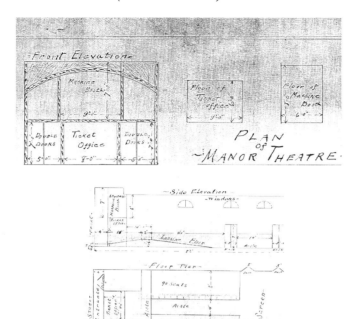

1910 DRAWINGS OF MANOR THEATRE BY B.M. YINGER

Contractor B. M. Yinger's 1910 drawings show a picture of how a Manor grocery store became a movie theatre. Carl Beretta tells the story of the bottom half of the building prior to the remodeling. He says the bottom floor of the theatre was originally used as a distribution business for imported foods. Then in 1938 his mother and father, Rose and John Beretta, opened a bar and restaurant in this part of the building. The most popular foods were their servings of oysters and a variety of Italian dishes. Eventually, this business was sold to Joe California who operated the restaurant as the Town Tavern "Side Pocket Bar" for many years.

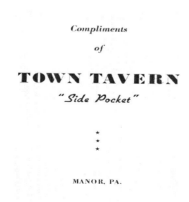

Advertisement courtesy - Firemen's Labor Day Program Book 1946

50b

Picture courtesy - Mrs. Patterson

SUNDAY SCHOOL PICNIC

Location was Brinkers Woods, where most picnics were held, including Sunday School outings.

Identified people are left to right: Curtis Brinker, Gertrude Altman(with ribbon), Clair Altman, Paul Beamer, Michael Beamer(above with beard), two unidentified individuals, Rev. Daughterty with 3 Noss girls in front, William Beamer, Mrs. Noss, Mrs. William Beamer, Lucy Beamer, Sam Heasley, Mrs. Larry Rankin with Louella & Eugene Rankin, Mrs. Millie Brinker, Mrs. Hiram Altman, and Catherine Yinger.

Picture courtesy - Mrs. Homer Naley

WESTMORELAND COAL CO. HOUSES

These company houses were owned and rented by the Westmoreland Coal Co., near the Biddle Mine west of Manor, near Brush Hill.

These double houses were rented to the miners who were employed at the nearby mine.

PAVING RACE STREET

A street paving scene on Race Street about the year 1907.

Prior to that time, all streets in Manor were of the dirt variety and most of the side-walks were made of boards.

The sewer lines were all laid before the paving operation.

Identified here, third man from the left, wearing a flat straw hat, is J. R. Sowash, owner and operator of the big store on the left.

LOOKING NORTH

This is a view (approximately 1914) looking north on Race Street from the railroad crossing. The small building on the left was the newsstand, run by Pappy Coulter. In back of the newsstand is a grocery store run by Dave Crock.

At the right corner is a red brick store building owned by Tom Miller, and behind it is the old Manor National Bank building.

Note the horse and buggy outfits.

JIMTOWN MINE

The Jimtown mine opened in the last half of the 1800's, and closed about the year 1920. It was located on the Manor Valley branch of the Pennsylvania Railroad, about 3/4 of a mile north of Manor.

The mine was a tipple type operation—the coal was brought to the surface by a system of cages or elevators. Two cages were operated in a system. As one cage was lowered to the pit bottom, the other cage was raised to the tipple floor level. These cages were raised and lowered by a large steel cable, suspended over two large slotted pulley wheels in the tipple roof, then ran from the pulley wheels down to the engine room nearby. These pulley wheels were about 8 feet in diameter.

These two large cables entering the engine room were wound and unwound on two large steel drums, slotted to handle the cables. The drums were controlled by a steam engine, which was fired by the boilers in the boiler room.

The operator, called the engineer's position, was in front of these drums, with the control arms about waist high and anchored to the floor. A large brass plate cut in the form of a half circle, stood in front of the operator, with a large hand mounted on the plate. This hand traveled from 0 to 180 degrees. This hand showed the operator the exact position of both cages in their up and down travel. At zero (0) degrees, one cage was at the bottom level, and the other cage was at tipple floor level. At 180 degrees the position of the cages was then reversed.

By this system, loaded coal cars came to the top, and empty mine cars were lowered to the pit bottom.

Air type signals or whistles controlled this operation from pit bottom - to tipple floor - to operator in the engine room.

As I was a paper delivery boy about this time, 1910, one of my morning routes covered Manor Hill, up to the Oak Street company houses, and down the dirt road that led past the mine office and tipple.

One of my must deliveries was to the mine office by 6:30 A.M.

The Jimtown mine was a pick and shovel operation, and the cars had to be moved constantly for hand loading. This was done by mules.

Jim Ferguson, from Harrison City, was mine superintendent, and he wanted to read the morning paper from 6:30 A.M. to 7 A.M.

Pappy Coulter was the owner of the newsstand, and his son Ernie Coulter, who at this time was a Vice President of the United States Steel plant at Cleveland, Ohio, enforced this rule of a 6:30 A.M. delivery of the morning paper to the mine office.

I always met this delivery, and later I had special privileges around the mine, being allowed up on the tipple floor and inside the engine room.

Inside the engine room Jim Ferguson had the operator, a man by the name of Fry, explain the control of the cages.

The mules were kept in large barns outside the mine and near the slope or roadway down into the mine. The mules, led by mule drivers, were led into the mine early in the morning, and came out of the mine late in the afternoon, by way of this slope.

This slope had some daylight at the entrance, about 30 or 40 yards, but from there on, it was midnight black.

The kids from Manor would go to the mine slope on workday afternoons and wait for the exit of the mules and miners. Standing at the slope entrance, they would wait, looking for a low flickering of light or a sound of some kind. Finally, the first flickering of light would appear, followed by more lights and then a steady stream of lights, showing that the mules and drivers were near the slope mouth. When the mules and drivers came within view, there was a quick exodus of kids over the fence to the nearby pasture. The reason for this was, when the mules and drivers surfaced to the outside, all 'H' would break loose.

The Jimtown mine and also the mine between Larimer and Ardara, had coke making operations, and commuters on the westbound railroad trains could observe the bee hive ovens in operation.

These ovens at the Jimtown mine were south of the tipple, and the remains of about 40 of these ovens are still in view today in 1976. No record was available when these bee hive ovens ceased operation, but the mine closed about 1920.

Here are three photos of Jimtown miners and mules, taken in the year 1913.

The four miners are (left to right): Charlie Wiltrek, George Sawish, Charlie Garr, and Albert Sawish.

The three drivers with two black and one white mules are (left to right): Albert Sawish, Charlie Wiltrek, and Charlie Garr.

The three drivers with three black mules are (left to right): Charlie Lewis, Nick Dzendzel, and John Atson.

On the miners caps are carbide lamps, used by miners at this time, and they all carried metal dinner buckets.

Pictures courtesy - Nick Dzendzel
Notes by Wayne A. Caldwell

COAL BUCKET HILL
JIMTOWN - OAK STREET EXTENSION

Coal Bucket Hill and Jimtown are names given to what is now Oak Street Extension. It became the home to families that came to America from Europe in the late 19th Century. Approximately ten of these families immigrated from Austria, Russia, the Ukraine, Poland and Croatia. They lived in homes extending up the hill from Oak and Fourth Streets to the end of Oak Street Extension.

GEORGE HEASLEY AT COKE OVEN 1989

The names Coal Bucket Hill and Jimtown were associated with the Jimtown mine, which was located north of the hill along the railroad tracks that stretched from Manor to Harrison City. Also along these tracks were a series of coke ovens used by the mines. The picture above shows one of the ovens that lined the hillside near the site of the Jimtown Manor Mine. Located here also, were two natural ponds used by Manor kids for ice-skating during the winter months.

At the corner of Oak and Fourth Streets, on the left side going up the hill, lived the Andrew Scheuerle family; next was the residence of Joseph Was, owner of the Was Brothers Garage. The Walter Scheuerle family was

next, and then Mike Baron's house, which was the last one situated on the bricked portion of the street.

Oak Street Extension was a narrow unpaved dirt road ending with the last house on the left side of the street. There were no houses on the right side of the road. On the right was a spring where everyone collected water. Paving the street became a project topic for Manor Borough Council in 1942.

OAK STREET BEFORE PAVING

Mr. Hammer was appointed to do a layout of the street.

The contract for grading, draining, and paving was awarded to Frank O. Patterson for $7,818.30. The work was held up by the water company, and then by the weather. The project was finally completed in 1943.

All of the houses, except two, were double-dwelling company houses similar to most "patch" houses of mining communities. Later, after the mines closed, the houses were purchased from the Westmoreland Coal Company. Some houses sold for as little as $1,200.00. You can identify these houses today as you drive up Oak Street.

THE DZENDZEL HOME 1925

The first house on the extension was the home of Mike Ropicky. Next in line were the Kotoks, the Dzendzels, the Adams, the Zierskis, and the Oleches owned the last house.

Nick Kotok was an Air Force pilot during the Korean War. He enjoyed greeting his family and neighbors on Oak Street hill with a fly-by. He flew low enough to wave, but high enough to miss the rooftops. It was thought that he would one day land in someone's kitchen. It was always a relief when the plane finally ascended.

THE DZENDZELS IN MANOR 1925

The Dzendzel family history began in Wisloczek, Austria where Nicholas, Sr. was born in 1891. Nicholas's wife Mary Prybyten was born in Ropyciaruska, Austria in 1895. They met in the United States and were married in 1917. Nicholas worked as a painter for the Pennsylvania Railroad. Eventually he and his wife settled on Oak Street where they raised five children: Nick, Jr., Steve, Mike, Helen, and Paul. They all attended Manor School.

OAK STREET IN JUNE 2005

Paul and Jean Dzendzel still live at the top of Oak Street near where Paul was raised. Their children grew up in Manor, and all attended Manor School. Paul's and Jean's daughter, Debbie Dzendzel Smolenski, one of the cashiers at Manor National Bank, lives on Oak Street down the hill from her parents. Debbie's children are the third generation in a family educated in the same community school, and fourth in lineage within a family that made Manor its home for more than eight decades.

PAUL AND JEAN DZENDZEL AT THEIR HOME
ON OAK STREET EXTENSION 2005

By Paul Dzendzel, George Heasley and Gail Noll.

TWO STORES OF J. W. SMELTZER

Located on Race Street and the corner of Observatory Street, the lots for these two stores were secured at the settlement of the Ludwick Estate.

The building at the left was built as a general store in approximately 1915, by Mr. J. W. Smeltzer. The building at the right was built by Mr. George Beamer in the same year, and was a general store.

The Beamer store was taken over by Mr. J. W. Smeltzer and both stores were operated by him, along with his two sons, James and Harry.

The early method of delivery was by horse and rig, followed by an auto van, as shown.

At the left corner is a curbside gasoline pump, which was the general practice at this time, as there were no drive-in stations.

This business thrived for many years at this location.

Picture courtesy - Mrs. Homer Naley

MEN'S BIBLE CLASS

On June 6, 1915, the Men's Bible Class of Manor attended a convention at Denmark-Manor Reformed Church.

There were 35 members in attendance. Their teacher, Zeff Burger, standing at extreme right, taught the Men's Bible Class at the Church for over 56 years.

Picture courtesy - Jake Miller

LOCAL MANOR INDEPENDENT BAND

A local Manor band was organized in the early 1900's. They were in attendance mostly at local celebrations, and also for town entertainment.

Identification: front row, left to right, Mr. Shotts, the band director; Mr. Hanna, Sr.; Bob Kline; John Stubbs; Ray Kline.

Back row, left to right, Clair Hanna; Bob Wilson; John Williams; Dyed Smith; Bob Bestwick; Carl Truxall; last two not identified.

Picture courtesy - Virginia Beamer Crum

FIREMAN'S LABOR DAY PARADE

The large structure in the center is the Sowash building.

The Tilbrook Hotel property, at right, with second floor porch, was used by John Anthony as a dairy store, garage, repair shop and filling station.

The Altman mill, having been dismantled, is the vacant lot where the cars are parked. This location later became the home of the Manor American Legion.

Picture courtesy - Mrs. Homer Naley

PICNIC DAY

The crowd on the railroad platform is awaiting arrival of the special picnic train to Idlewild Park, in the early 1920's.

The Manor merchants sponsored this annual picnic, and the Manor community always looked forward to it.

The kids loved the ride to Idlewild Park, as it gave them a chance to go through the long, dark Radebaugh railroad tunnel and also on to ride the Ligonier Valley Railroad.

In the background, is the Manor passenger and freight station with about four freight cars parked on the siding.

MANOR - WESTMORELAND CITY
COMMUNITY PICNIC

The Manor – Westmoreland City Community Picnic has been an annual event for 85 years. Efforts to gather the earliest history of it have been fruitless. Even with talking to the oldest citizens, I came up empty handed. My only clues have been pictures dated 1920, which show the crowds awaiting the special train to take them to Idlewild Park.

This I do know. Paul Beamer was a personal friend of the McDonald family who owned Idlewild Park. It was Paul who was responsible for organizing the first community picnic. It must have been a success as it really took off from there. Countless people have worked together over the years to keep it a successful event.

Some of the earlier General Chairmen were: Luther Mitchell, John Sofko, Al Kukovich, and Regis Holden. The means to finance the picnic have remained the same. Our good citizens are asked to give the money for prizes. In the past, coin cards were filled with quarters to total $5.00. The coin card committee members were responsible for distribution, collection and counting of the coin cards. Early picnic prizes were household or personal items.

This method has been changed for at least the 13 years since I have been the General Chairman. We now use a ticket, which the donor signs. The ticket shows the amount contributed. Each solicitor has a tally sheet on which the donations are recorded. Donor names are drawn at the Park. We give only cash prizes and this seems to be a drawing card now. All prizes except the donor card prizes must be claimed at the park. Any unclaimed prize is forfeited and the money returns to the treasury.

Everyone seems to enjoy the picnic. The date is always set for the last Thursday of July. Some families set vacations to be in Manor for the picnic. Our solicitors say people tell them they look forward to this annual event.

By General Chairperson, Enid Walter

Courtesy - Mrs. Elsie Lauffer

DR. SHIREY

In the early 1900's Manor had two doctors in town, Dr. Shirey, who is shown here, and Dr. A. D. Miller.

It looks like a little tom-foolery going on, as the doctor is holding a rope tied to the front axle, with a slight grin on his face.

This hand crank model, with a brass bar from the front end to center of the windshield, must be a 1908 model.

In view here are utility buildings in the rear of the doctor's home.

At this same location today, is the Manor United States Post Office Building.

DOCTOR CHARLES SHIREY

If anyone reading this story has ever seen the old TV show "Gunsmoke" you will recall the character of "Doc". Well, Manor had its own "Doc." Anyone who ever met Dr. Charles Shirey will tell you that the TV character must have been modeled after him.

Doc Shirey was probably the person in town most known and recognized by everyone in Manor. He was from the Youngstown area of Westmoreland County and began his adult life as a school teacher, in order to earn his way to his dream of becoming a physician. He and his wife, Emily, moved to Manor in 1872 –1873, and he began his practice of medicine. They designed and built the house in which they lived, and he practiced. A photo of this house is in this book. There were three entrances, Race Street, Doctor's Office, and back porch.

In the early days of his practice, he traveled all over the Manor area in his horse and buggy. As population grew and the need for doctor's services increased, he kept up to date by trading in his horse and buggy for a Plymouth Coupe. It was a familiar sight to see Doc Shirey on his way to a house call. As decades rolled along, so did Doc in his free wheeling Hupmobile, then his Dodge Fluid Drive. The horse stable in the yard quickly gave way to a two-car garage.

Edward "Ted" Miller worked for Dr. Shirey, first cleaning the spring house and the stable then doing the gardening. When Doc moved from horse and buggy to automobile he took young Miller with him on house calls. When Doc made his house call, he instructed his young companion to "turn the car around." This is how Ted learned to drive. Eventually, he became the Shirey's chauffeur. When Doc Shirey died, he willed his Dodge Fluid Drive to Ted. It was Ted's first car. The remaining part of the estate was willed to the Lutheran Children's Home in Greenville, Pa.

Doc Shirey was a member of the first School Board in Manor, and sat on the board of the Manor National Bank.

Because of his farming background, Doc's hobby was horticulture. He grew a wide variety of vegetables. His garden was beautiful, filled with roses, narcissus, gladiolus, and hollyhocks. They were so impressive that his wife, Emily, wrote a poem about these beautiful blooms, titled, "Hollyhock Row". The poem can be read in this book.

Doc Shirey was a talented and busy man, one of Manor's most well known and beloved residents.

By Dorothy Y. Miller and Nancy Miller

MANOR POST OFFICE

This is the inside of the Manor Post Office in the year 1921. The office was located in the old bank building, which site is now the parking lot of the new bank building.

In the picture are (left to right): Virginia Beamer, Sarah Caldwell and James Beamer, the Postmaster.

LEATHERS STORE - LABOR DAY 1919

This location is directly across from Borough parking lot and houses the Joe Crock cleaning business and O'Bryan's appliances.

LABOR DAY 1919 AND WELCOME HOME DAY

World War I ended November 11, 1918 and the troops started coming home from Europe in 1919.

Thru the cooperation of the Manor Fire Department and all the town's business people, a giant Welcome Home Celebration was planned for Labor Day 1919.

This picture shows the women's medical team, two military men from out of town, and James Beamer.

The women in the picture are from left to right: Mrs. James Beamer, Mrs. J. P. Wilson, Mrs. Harry Cope, Miss Dorothy Traugher, Mrs. C. C. Walthour, and Mrs. John Steiner.

The two military men, identity unknown, were the speakers of the day, and on the right is James Beamer, officer in the Manor Fire Department.

SOUVENIR PROGRAM

MANOR'S
Annual Labor Day
Celebration

Held By
Manor Volunteer Fire Department

Monday, September 7th, 1925

Firemen's Labor Day Program Book 1925

Picture courtesy - Andy Lomicka

MILITARY FUNERAL PROCESSION OF
CARL LEROY McKELVEY

World War I ended on November 11, 1918, which, from that time on was known as Armistice Day, until recently when it was changed to Veterans Day.

Returning by boat, a slow process, it took a year or more for all the troops to get home from France and scattered parts of Europe.

Some of the veterans killed in action were sent back to the United States, but many were buried in cemeteries in France.

This military funeral, with horse drawn caisson, is moving to the Brush Creek Cemetery.

When the Manor American Legion Post was built, it was named in honor of Carl Leroy McKelvey.

CARL LEROY MCKELVEY

KILLED IN ACTION JULY 30, 1918
IN THE BATTLE OF THE MARNE

Carl Leroy McKelvey was killed in action on July 30, 1918 at Chateau Thierry, France. Manor American Legion Post 472 is named in his honor.

MEMORIAL DAY SERVICE – BRUSH CREEK CEMETARY
AT THE GRAVE SITE OF CARL LEROY MCKELVEY

John R. Naley, also a veteran of World War I, knew there were many other veterans in the Manor area and felt the need to organize an American Legion Post. There were 46 charter members. The first year they held bingo parties to raise funds. They also held a Memorial Day Service in the Reformed Church to honor those who had fallen in battle. Prior to World War II, they held an annual Thanksgiving Raffle in C. P. Lauffer's garage with live chickens and turkeys as prizes.

MANOR AMERICAN LEGION 2005

With the donation of the ground by the Altman family, construction of the current building began in 1947. Many of the Legionnaires did the construction work, painting, and plumbing, etc. The first public function to be held in the completed second floor was held on Memorial Day, May 25, 1952.

After the gymnasium was built in the American Legion Post 472 Home, it ushered in a basketball program unequaled by the state. Programs were provided for boys from ages 6 to 14. The legion also sponsored a senior team, which was entered in the prestigious Pittsburgh Honus Wagner League.

Edward Hoak was elected State Commander in 1960 and Virginia Holden was elected state President in 1967. Serving as county commanders were: Adam Fisher, James Kelly, Hector Sproat, Donald Nicholson, Floyd Sheasley and James Grimaldi.

MEMORIAL GARDEN

On November 8, 1971 the Memorial Garden on Race Street across from Manor National Bank was dedicated. It was made possible by contributions of organizations and citizens of Manor. It was built to honor servicemen and women from the Manor area that served in the armed forces.

THE AMERICAN LEGION'S INVOLVEMENT EXTENDED TO THE MANOR SCHOOL

ESSAY AWARD WINNER — Manor American Legion Commander Floyd Sheasley, left, and Donald Nicholson, right, state chairman of the Pennsylvania American Legion Essay-Contest, presented an award Monday night to Lori Lane, center, local winner of the contest. The theme of the essay is titled: "What Being a United States Veteran Means." Lane, daughter of Mr. and Mrs. Dennis Lane of Broadway Street, Manor, is a student at Hempfield Senior High School.

CARL LEROY MCKELVEY POST 472 AWARDS

The PA Department of the Legion sponsors an Essay contest every year. For many years, Don Nicholson served as State Chairman. Many Manor students have been awarded prizes in local, district and tri-district contests. The Awards have traditionally been presented at a special assembly in the School. It is a much coveted award.

PRESENTATION OF THE AMERICAN LEGION 8TH GRADE AWARD

Beginning in 1935 this Manor Post 472 began presenting the outstanding student award to an outstanding boy in the 8th grade class. Soon after, the Auxiliary began to present an award to the outstanding girl. These awards are based on honor, leadership, Americanism, scholarship, and service to others. A plaque with the names of the recipients was placed in the school. When the Junior High moved from Manor to West Hempfield, the awards continued to be presented there. This year, 2005, has been the 70th consecutive year of award presentation.

By Don and Betty Nicholson

MANOR AMERICAN LEGION CLUB ROOM 1962

In the 1960's Manor Legion was the place to be on Saturday nights. The two orchestras that drew the largest crowds were *Frankie's Trio* and *Jack Tady's Orchestra.* The parking lot was always filled, and if you lived "up Observatory" you knew not to leave home on Saturday night! You weren't getting through town easily because of cars and people on Race Street going to the Legion.

Manor American Legion started a mixed-chorus in 1959 under the direction of Bob Bevan. It performed in American Legion Homes throughout Westmoreland and Allegheny Counties. Manor Legion was the only Legion Home in the southwestern region of Pennsylvania to have a mixed-chorus.

MANOR AMERICAN LEGION MIXED CHORUS   BOB BEVAN,
                                        DIRECTOR

Contributions from Post 472 and the Ladies Auxiliary supported the chorus by providing money to purchase music and a place to practice. With *Frankie's Trio* the Chorus entertained 150 veterans at the VA Hospital in Oakland.

When Westinghouse Electric Co. moved Bob Bevan to North Carolina, he was replaced as director by Tom Cummins. At the same time, the accompanist, pianist Donna Kunkle, replaced Phyllis McDowell. In late 1961 the Chorus disbanded.

Manor American Legion Post 472 Ladies Auxiliary
25th Anniversary Party
June 10th 1960
Mixed-Chorus Program

It's a Grand Night for Singing
Happy Anniversary
Rose of No Man's Land (Solo by Frieda Harrison)
Carol of Belles
A Good Man is Hard to Find (Solo by Avis Altman)
So In Love
MacNamarra's Band (Solo by Clarence Anderson)
Give Me Your Tired Your Poor
Foolish Memories (Solo by Bob Bevan)
Real Nice Clambake
Sleep

By Avis Altman

Picture courtesy - Edith Cline

CHEVROLET DEALER ON RACE STREET

This was one of the early automobile dealerships located in Manor.

This Chevrolet agency, conducted by Sam Butler, was located on South Race Street.

The Chevrolet shown here was a model with a cloth top and clincher tires. The large automobile companies did not use steel tops until about 1920-1921.

Chevrolet nameplates can be seen on both cars.

Sam Butler is standing by the large model, with Charles Butler seated in the mini model.

This location was once occupied by the John Pierson Variety Store, the F. King Confectionery Store, the Sam Butler Chevrolet Agency and later by the Butler Fruit Market. Today it is occupied by the Elsie Lauffer Taxi and Confectionery and the Karen Lauffer Beauty Shop.

MANOR BOROUGH COUNCIL - 1927

Front row, left to right: Frank Steiner, C. P. Stahl, Matt Gray.

Back row, left to right: Bert Crock, Frank Ferree, Ford Heasley, and D. H. Caldwell-Burgess.

LABOR DAY 1927

Antique auto show? No, not so, as this was Labor Day in Manor in 1927.

Athletic events were in progress. The grandstand and bleachers shown here were nearly always crowded for baseball games, which were very popular at this time.

SUBWAY CONSTRUCTION UNDER THE
MANOR VALLEY RAILROAD

Subway excavation and construction at the Manor end of the railroad, required the removal of a large amount of earth, a part of which was used as the railroad bed for the Manor Valley branch and also the first waiting station for this railroad.

The first waiting room was located behind Buster Walter's newsstand.

The small station at the right, close to the trees, was the second waiting station.

The construction, which started in 1926 and completed in 1927, was to eliminate the dangerous railroad crossings, on which there were many deaths, cars destroyed, and beer wagons hit.

In two years, the active Manor Borough Council of 1926-27 accomplished all of the above.

SUBWAY CONSTRUCTION

Excavation had to be made here for the underpass under the Manor Valley Railroad, and also concurrently for the underpass on the main line of the Pennsylvania Railroad.

After the completion of the underpasses, all new streets had to be connected to the older ones.

Black building at far right, had been used as a petroleum depot by the Freedom Oil Company.

This depot, was serviced by a siding from the Manor Valley Railroad and tank cars were shifted to this siding for unloading.

BIRDSEYE VIEW

This birdseye view of Manor was taken in the late 1930's, from high up on Hill Street.

ROAD AND BRIDGE CONSTRUCTION

A new bridge over Brush Creek is shown here, with road grading being done in the background. A new concrete road was laid, and it followed the old dirt road and West Penn Street car line out of Manor and continued on to Penn and Jeannette.

The large structure in the background, at one time was known as the Dual-Tone. This name came from the trade name of the phonographs that were manufactured in this building by the Phonograph and Mfg. Co. All phonographs made here had a nameplate which stated "Manufactured by DUAL-TONE, Phonograph and Mfg. Co., Manor, Pa." Inside the lid they were also labeled "The King of Phonographs."

This building was originally a planing mill operated by Mr. Baer, and later by the Kemerer-Moore Co. When the phonograph business was discontinued, it was converted back to a planing mill by J. E. Myers.

Picture courtesy - Andy Lomicka

LOMICKA MARKET

The early Lomicka market on Race Street was located in the big H. A. Lauffer building, later occupied by J. R. Sowash stores.

Later, having acquired the property of Emanuel Crum, an addition was made to the front of this residence, to house a meat market, barber shop, and apartments.

The location is now occupied by the office of Manor Borough tax collector.

This market was later moved to a location beside Brush Creek.

Identified in the picture, (left to right) Andy Lomicka, owner, Glen Hockenberry, Cuddy Palmer, Heasley, and Cox.

ANDY LOMICKA 1991

Ninty-four year old Andy Lomicka is seen here selling Chance Tickets for the Fireman's Labor Day Celebration.

Picture courtesy - Dr. Charles Snyder Jr.

DOCTOR CHARLES SNYDER

A lifetime of medical practice was served by Dr. Charles Snyder Sr., to the residents of Manor and other surrounding communities.

After completing his schooling at Edinboro State Teachers College, he taught school at Helltown for a period in the late 1800's. Later he taught school at Westmoreland City, and at this time roomed with Sam and Annie Schroder.

Leaving the teaching profession, he went back to college, changing his profession from teaching to medicine. While he was in medical school, a large group of Manor citizens requested by letter, that he come and serve this community as Resident Physician. In his reply, he stated that one more year was needed to finish his schooling.

After completing school, he started his practice in Manor, having his first residence and office in the J. R. Sowash building, on Race Street, about 1918.

At this period of time, a nationwide flue epidemic, called the Killer Flu, swept across the country and there were thousands of deaths. The demand for medical attention during this flu epidemic was never ending.

Later, Dr. Charles Snyder Sr., moved to a location on North Railroad Street, known as the Harry Bisel property, where he completed his medical practice.

Two sons of Dr. Charles Snyder Sr., grew up to follow in their father's footsteps in the medical profession. Dr. Wilson Snyder located in Sharon, Pa., and Dr. Charles Snyder Jr., located in Manor, at first in the Manor National Bank building, and later at his father's residence on North Railroad Street. He was later appointed administrator for the Jeannette District Memorial Hospital for many years.

Photo Courtesy - Frank Pink

CHRIST WALTHOUR HOLDS FAMILY
BAPTISMAL CERTIFICATE

Greensburg attorney Christ Walthour holds a Walthour
Family Baptismal Certificate, written in German, dated 1803.
The Certificate, one of the oldest documents of its kind
found in Westmoreland County, is preserved in the archives
of the County Historical Society.

About half of the original settlers and the first ministers
of Westmoreland County were of German extraction and
heritage.

Most of the early baptismal certificates and other
documents were written in German.

It was about 1850 before the German language was
phased out of the market place.

CHRISTOPHER C. WALTHOUR JR.

"Christy" Walthour was born December 3, 1916 in a house that still stands at the corner of Broadway and Atlantic Streets in Manor, the son of Christopher C. Sr. and Bessie T. (McKee) Walthour.

Christy was educated at Manor School and after graduation from Greensburg High School, he attended the University of Pittsburgh, and graduated in 1939. He then enrolled in the University of Pittsburgh School of Law, graduating in 1942. In 1943, he entered into the U.S. Army and completed Army Administration School O.C.S. #3, at which time he accepted a commission in the Army of the United Sates. He attained the rank of captain and served his country for several years as a prosecutor in the Japanese War Crimes Trials. He was a decorated Veteran of World War II.

For 43 years, he practiced law with his partner, Robert Wm. Garland, in a law firm (now known as Walthour and Garland, Attorneys at Law, Greensburg), which had been founded by Christ's father, C.C. Walthour Sr., in the early years of the last century. After his discharge from the Army, he returned to Greensburg to pursue his law practice, which he continued until his death.

As an attorney, he was respected as a knowledgeable and tenacious litigator and a true gentleman in and out of the courtroom. He was a member of the Westmoreland, Pennsylvania, and American Bar

Associations, was admitted to practice before the Pennsylvania Supreme Court, the Pennsylvania Superior Court, the Commonwealth Court, and various other state courts, as well as the U.S. Supreme Court and various federal courts. He was a member of the American College of Trial Lawyers and the Westmoreland Academy of Trial Lawyers.

It was said that he "lived, ate, and drank the law." He was known as a formidable attorney, but had a "gentle quality and a generous side." He was known to be economical in his habits, but extremely generous in the giving of time and talents.

In addition to the practice of law, he was president of the Manor National Bank from 1947 to 2003, he served on the board of Manor Public Library of which his mother, Bessie Walthour, was a founding member. He was a member of Shidle Lodge 601 F&AM, the Shrine Syria Temple, and the Valley of Pittsburgh Consistory.

He assisted many community organizations: The Manor Volunteer Fire Company, the Manor United Church of Christ, and Manor Borough. Many individuals, families, friends, and community members benefited from his legal skills and professional knowledge.

In the last years of his life, he mentored and began interacting with students at the University of Pittsburgh Law School, having been invited by Pitt to share his life and legal experiences. Mr. Walthour died August 15, 2003. He was posthumously inducted into the University of Pittsburgh Cathedral of Learning Society in 2005.

Attorney John Scales was quoted saying, "My father always told us that it is important to pattern ourselves after someone with the highest moral standards, and you cannot do better than Christy Walthour."

By Dorothy Y. Miller and Nancy Miller

THE DR. SHIREY HOME

This photo of the Dr. Shirey home was taken from Race St. The man under the canopy is standing at what was the entrance to Dr. Shirey's office. To the right of the pole is the present location of the Manor National Bank Parking Lot. At the rear of the home was the Kifer Farm Spring House, built of stone exterior and oak timber inside, mortised and pegged. Carved on one of the oak timbers inside was the year 1809. Joe Hurst was the last owner and occupant of this home before it was dismantled, to be replaced by the present Manor Post Office.

Illustration courtesy - Emily Munson Shirey

TRANSPORTATION

The very first transportation around the vicinity of Manor was by horse or horse and buggy.

In 1852, the railroad came through Manor, but no records are available as to how well they served the community.

In the 1890's, the West Penn Railways Co., established a traction line from Greensburg to Irwin. Their service was based on a street car running at half hour intervals. They had a service from Irwin to Trafford, and one from Greensburg to Connellsville, and a line that ran to Latrobe. They also established a freight service from Pittsburgh to Trafford on the Pittsburgh line, then from Trafford to Greensburg on the West Penn Lines. West Penn also operated a line from Irwin to McKeesport.

West Penn Traction furnished car service to two amusement parks in the summertime, namely Oakford Park, and Olympia Park, which is now the location of the Olympia shopping center. This summer service to these parks was in open air cars.

This traction service from Greensburg to Irwin came to a halt on July 13, 1952.

Benjamin Rush Walthour, who was born in Hempfield Township close by Manor Station, grew up on the farm, later learned the carpenter trade and in 1877, he opened a livery stable on South Race Street, Manor. He operated this livery for many years, and upon his death in 1903, this livery stable business was taken over by his son Howard Cherry Walthour.

Later this livery business was taken over by Eli Kistler and J. R. Sowash. Eli Kistler being a Funeral Director, offered a complete horse drawn funeral, with hearse and carriages.

Another livery business was located next to this Walthour livery, and was run by Nevin McElfresh. These livery stables were later dismantled in the early 1900's.

By 1900, the commuter railroad service was well established between Pittsburgh and Greensburg.

The Pennsylvania Railroad built many branch lines after the coal mines started operating in 1860 and years to follow. A branch line ran from Greensburg to Connellsville, Uniontown and Fairchance. This line hauled coal and coke, as well as having a passenger service.

A branch line was built at the Radebaugh Station to haul out the coal from the big Arona mine and the Herminie No. 2 mine.

A branch line was built out of Irwin called the Sewickley Valley Branch. This line hauled coal from the Adams mine and also had a passenger service.

A branch was built from Trafford to Export, to service the large Export mine, and this branch also had a passenger service.

The Manor Valley Railroad was built to haul coal from the Claridge mine and the Jimtown mine. Later, another mine was opened at McCullough on the Manor Valley Line.

The Pennsylvania Railroad had a large commuter service in this area due to the heavy industry up and down the valley.

A copy of the train schedule (westbound) issued on November 27, 1910 follows:

Train No.	Train Name	Leave Manor	Arrive Pittsburgh
281	Greensburg Ac.	6:13 A.M.	7:12 A.M.
285	Greensburg Ac.	6:31 A.M.	7:36 A.M.
283	Derry Ac.	7:29 A.M.	8:28 A.M.
295	Greensburg Ex.	8:01 A.M.	8:56 A.M.
287	Pittsburgh Ac.	8:39 A.M.	9:42 A.M.
33	Pittsburgh Ac.	11:26 A.M.	12:30 P.M.
291	Greensburg Ac.	12:42 P.M.	1:40 P.M.
293	Pittsburgh Ac.	2:38 P.M.	3:38 P.M.
41	Way Passenger	4:55 P.M.	6:00 P.M.
113	Greensburg Ac.	6:52 P.M.	7:44 P.M.
95	Pittsburgh Ac.	7:30 P.M.	8:33 P.M.
955	Greensburg Ac.	10:17 P.M.	11:20 P.M.
299	Greensburg Ac.	11:56 P.M.	12:56 P.M.

The abbreviations, Ac means accommodation, and Ex means express. By this schedule, train No. 113 ran to Pittsburgh in 52 minutes, and train No. 295 ran to Pittsburgh in 55 minutes.

The eastbound schedule on November 27, 1910 was as follows:

Train No.	Train Name	Leave Pittsburgh	Arrive Manor
92	Harrisburg Ex.	4:30 A.M.	5:25 A.M.
100	Uniontown Ac.	5:38 A.M.	6:35 A.M.
12	Mainline Ex.	7:12 A.M.	8:02 A.M.
102	Yough Ex.	8:20 A.M.	9:17 A.M.
298	Greensburg Ac.	9:45 A.M.	10:50 A.M.
280	Blairsville Ex.	10:40 A.M.	11:38 A.M.
104	Uniontown Ex.	12:25 P.M.	1:16 P.M.
282	Greensburg Ac.	2:00 P.M.	2:50 P.M.
284	Johnstown Ac.	3:34 P.M.	4:41 P.M.
96	Harrisburg Ex.	4:48 P.M.	5:51 P.M.
288	Greensburg Ac.	5:28 P.M.	6:20 P.M.
290	Derry Ac.	5:30 P.M.	6:35 P.M.
954	Greensburg Ac.	7:25 P.M.	8:27 P.M.
4	Philadelphia Ex.	8:33 P.M.	9:22 P.M.
294	Greensburg Ac.	10:00 P.M.	10:53 P.M.
296	Greensburg Ac.	11:40 P.M.	12:31 A.M.

This last train, No. 296 leaving Pittsburgh at 11:40 P.M., and due to arrive at Manor at 12:31 A.M., was called the 'Bummer', probably because the riders on this train were bumming around Pittsburgh all day. This 'Bummer' train was always crowded.

The little old Manor Valley Railroad had a schedule of its own, too.

SOUTHWARD

Train No. 328	Leave Claridge 8:10 A.M.	Arrive Manor	8:30 A.M.
Train No. 330	Leave Claridge 4:02 P.M.	Arrive Manor	4:20 P.M.

NORTHWARD

Train No. 339	Leave Manor 9:20 A.M.	Arrive Claridge 9:42 A.M.
Train No. 331	Leave Manor 5:00 P.M.	Arrive Claridge 5:13 P.M.

No time schedule was given here for the inbetween stations of Harrison City and Clarks Crossing.

A Bus line was established in 1919 by Elmer Dudley, a resident of Shafton. This Bus line ran from Manor to Westmoreland City, to Shafton, Irwin, Jacktown, Circleville and to Stewartsville. This Bus line was the first area line to operate by the permission of a Pennsylvania Public Utilities Commission Certificate.

Elmer Dudley operated this line until 1923, and then this line was transferred to David Magill. The Magill family operates this giant Lincoln Coach Line today.

Picture courtesy - Virginia Beamer Crum

MANOR VALLEY RAILROAD

One of the very early locomotives on the Manor Valley Railroad on one single track at Clarks Crossing, a station between Harrison City and Claridge.

OLD MANOR VALLEY ENGINE

The old engine plus two wooden coaches, running several trips a day, was the railroad passenger service between Manor, Harrison City, Clark's Crossing, and Claridge in the late 1800's and early 1900's. This spur of the Pennsylvania railroad was built after 1860 to haul coal which was being mined at Claridge, later at Jimtown mine, and still later at the McCullough mine.

This old engine, hauling two cars, made the first trip in the morning from Claridge to Manor delivering milk in 5 gallon and 10 gallon cans to be shipped to Pittsburgh.

All the farmers in the Denmark-Manor district delivered the milk early in the morning to the platforms at the stations of Claridge, Clark's Crossing, and Harrison City. It was unloaded at Manor on to hand trucks at the Valley Station platform, which was built on a high fill of earth on the same level as the main line railroad. Here the milk was loaded on the milk train for delivery to the Pittsburgh market. Whenever the milk train stopped at Manor, at approximately 9:00 A.M., it took quite a while before the train could leave the station as the loading of the many cans was a time consuming operation.

The coming of the automobile and truck ended this hauling of milk by railroad, and later the Manor Valley train was discontinued.

Picture courtesy – Joe Rigney

Picture courtesy - Mrs. Elmer G. Schade

MANOR BRANCH TRAIN

This train, complete with a seven man crew, was composed of one wooden passenger coach, and one combination passenger, baggage, mail, express and freight coach. It made two complete round trips between Manor and Claridge on every week day, and served the two inbetween stations of Harrison City and Clarks Crossing.

Joe Rigney, a life long railroader, working as a telegrapher for the Pennsylvania Railroad, could identify years ago, this 7 man crew, but time has a way of playing tricks with your memory.

COAL TRAIN ENTERING THE
MANOR VALLEY RAILROAD

Early in the 1900's, when the Jimtown and Claridge mines were operating, this scene was repeated about twice a week.

A long line of empty coal cars were hauled to the sidings, adjacent to the mine openings or tipples, where in a day by day operation, they were loaded, and hauled out to the main line, and then to the coal market.

Most of the coal production in Westmoreland County was handled on spurs or branch lines built by the Pennsylvania Railroad.

RAILROAD EXCURSION TICKET

In the late 1800's and the first half of the 1900's, Pennsylvania Railroad passenger transportation was at its peak, and as many as 21 passenger trains a day stopped at Manor to receive and discharge passengers.

Shown here, is a two day excursion ticket, to be used within two days as indicated by station date stamp on back of ticket, between Manor and Irwin. Note the Manor Ticket Office stamp on back of ticket dated April 26, 1890. Cost of this return trip ticket not available, but a guess would be 10 cents in those days.

DIRT ROAD AND WEST PENN LINE TO JEANNETTE

Looking east from Manor in the mid 1900's, we see the West Penn Traction Lines and the old dirt road leading to Penn and Jeannette.

TINKER TOWN

As you leave Manor on the road to Penn just before you get to Wegley Hollow is the area of Manor known as Tinker Town. It had 28 houses and one foundation as the lived-in-basement of a future house used to be called. The area's name came from an original resident that earned his living as a tinker. A tinker sharpened scissors and knives and was a mender of pots, pans, umbrellas, and countless other household items. Tinkers carried all their tools on their backs including the grinding wheel. They used a contraption like back pack straps to hold it all.

PENN/MANOR ROAD NEAR TINKER TOWN 2005

The first row of houses was so close to the trolley track running along the road that residents could virtually step off their porches onto the tracks. The tracks were located where the car in the picture is parked. The West Penn Trolley ran about every 30 minutes. Because Tinker Town was in Hempfield Township, the children went to Wegley Elementary School. Many of the children from the Jones, King, Loughner, and Nedley families were very active in the Manor Methodist Church. I fondly recall one resident, Mr. Jones, who had a fine pack of coon dogs, which he would use at night to coon hunt.

By Dick Hauser

BUSINESS IN MANOR

The following is a list of business and professional people, who were located in and around Manor Station, later Manor Borough, in the last half of the 1800's, and the first 40 years in the 1900's. These listings were taken from the New York Industrial Recorder, the Interior Business Directory, from old newspaper clippings and magazines. No records were available as to the beginning and ending of each business.

WALTHOUR GRIST MILL	Brush Creek
KIFER AND PAINTER MILL	Manor Station
M. BEAMER AND SON HANDLE FACTORY	Manor Station
BAER AND POOL PLANING MILL	South Railroad Street
P. R. BRINKER PLANING MILL	Manor Station
GREENAWALT BROS. PLANING MILL	Race Street
JOHN HARVEY GENERAL MERCHANDISE	Race Street
M. ISETT HARNESS MAKER	Race Street
M. HIPPARD GENERAL STORE	Race Street
BART HOLMES, BLACKSMITH	Race Street
HERMAN KOOSER, BLACKSMITH AND WAGON MAKER	Race Street
HARRY STEINER, DUCK FARM - PLANING MILL	Manor
P. R. BRINKER AND SONS, GENERAL STORE	Race Street
STANLEY AUSLANDER, JEWELER AND WATCHMAKER	Race Street
C. BRINKER GENERAL STORE	Race Street
W. F. BRINKER, HARDWARE	Race Street
MRS. E. M. BEST, SHOES	Race Street
FRANK PENMAN, SHOES	Race Street
FREEDOM OIL CO., M. B. WALKER	Manor
J. A. BURGER, GROCERIES	Race Street
BURGER BROS., SEWING MACHINES	Race Street
WM. GARLAND, CONFECTIONERY	Railroad & Race Streets
M. E. GRIFFITH, PHYSICIAN	Railroad Street
B. M. YINGER, APIARY	Manor
DR. LYDIA, PHYSICIAN	Railroad Street
F. L. FRY, DRUGGIST	Race Street
HOMER NALEY, DRUGGIST	Race Street
G. W. CROCK, GENERAL STORE	Race Street
COMMERCIAL HOTEL, J. L. FLAHERTY, PROP.	Race Street
HOTEL POOL, S. A. STOUFFER, PROP.	Railroad & Race Streets
DOUGLASS HOTEL	Race Street
MAYER HOTEL	Race Street
McWILLIAMS HOTEL	Race Street
KEMERER MOORE PLANING MILLS	Railroad Street
H. A. LAUFFER, GENERAL STORE	Race Street
J. R. SOWASH, GENERAL STORE	Race Street
H. F. LUDWIG, JUSTICE OF THE PEACE	Race Street
P. H. NALEY, JUSTICE OF THE PEACE	Race Street
MANOR OBSERVER NEWSPAPER - 1880-1890	Manor
ALTMAN AND GOEHRING, GENERAL STORE	Race Street
MANOR VALLEY ROLLING MILLS McWILLIAMS & ALTMAN	Race Street
J. MATHIAS & CO., DISTILLERY	Manor
R. J. McLANAHAN, TINWARE & STOVES	Race Street
HIGHBERGER, TINNING & ROOFING	Race Street
McCLELLAND BROOM CO.	Second Street
H. S. NALEY, BAKERY	Observatory & Race Streets
FRANK BEITER HOTEL	Race Street
GRESSLER HOTEL	Race Street

TILBROOK HOTEL . . . . Race Street
M. A. NALEY, TINWARE & STOVES . . . . Race Street
I. BAER DRUGSTORE . . . . Race Street
W. J. SNYDER STORE . . . . Race Street
P. WAUGAMAN STORE . . . . Race Street
C. R. HEASLEY, GENERAL STORE . . . . North Railroad Street
MILLER GRAINERY . . . . Railroad Street
DR. MILLER, PHYSICIAN . . . . Railroad Street
DR. C. SNYDER, SR., PHYSICIAN . . . . Race Street
HEINTZELMAN HOTEL . . . . Railroad Street
J. SIMMONDS HOTEL . . . . Railroad Street
STICKELS DAIRY . . . . Manor
ANDY RAMSEY, CIGAR FACTORY . . . . Railroad Street
C. P. STAHL, CIGAR FACTORY . . . . Railroad Street
J. E. MYERS, PLANING MILL . . . . South Railroad Street
DUAL-TONE, PHONOGRAPHS . . . . South Railroad Street
PETE NATION MEAT MARKET . . . . Race Street
ALGY POOL MEAT MARKET . . . . Race Street
JOHN PIERSON, STORE & RESTAURANT . . . . North Railroad Street
JOHN PIERSON CONFECTIONERY . . . . Race Street
KING CONFECTIONERY . . . . Race Street
S. H. SCHMIDT, JEWELER & WATCHMAKER . . . . Race Street
C. J. SKELLY, PHYSICIAN . . . . Railroad Street
MELLONS DAIRY . . . . Manor
MANOR ELECTRIC LIGHT CO. . . . . South Railroad Street
THE MANOR NEWS, GRANT HELMAN, ED. . . . . Race Street
G. B. ROOF, SHOEMAKER . . . . Cor. Race & Railroad Streets
C. A. SHIREY, PHYSICIAN . . . . Race Street
GEORGE HIGGINS, BARBER . . . . Race Street
DICK KELLNER, BARBER . . . . Race Street
W. H. WAUGAMAN, DENTIST . . . . Race Street
DR. KING, DENTIST . . . . Race Street
CHARS. SIMPSON, BARBER . . . . Race Street
NELL HOLLEY, TONSORIAL . . . . Railroad Street
MANOR NEWSSTAND, J. COULTER . . . . Race Street
B. RUSH WALTHOUR, LIVERY . . . . Race Street
NEVIN McELFRESH, LIVERY . . . . Race Street
FRANK HEASLEY, GENERAL STORE . . . . Race Street
J. P. WILSON, GENERAL STORE . . . . Race Street
J. W. SMELTZER, GENERAL STORE . . . . Race Street
GEORGE BEAMER, GENERAL STORE . . . . Race Street
DR. CHARLES SNYDER, SR., PHYSICIAN . . . . Race & North Railroad Streets
DR. CHARLES SNYDER, JR., PHYSICIAN . . . . Race & North Railroad Streets
TONY CAMPAGNA, SHOEMAKER . . . . Observatory Street
PETE PIAZZA, SHOEMAKER . . . . Race Street
M. L. SHRADER, BARBER . . . . Race Street
KEYSTONE STORES . . . . Race Street
P. H. BUTLER STORES . . . . Race Street
CLOVER FARM STORES . . . . Race Street
LOMICKA BROS., MEAT MARKET . . . . Race Street
ORION PINKERTON, MEAT MARKET . . . . Race Street
MIKE PALIMASANO, FRUIT MARKET . . . . Race Street
SAM BUTLER, CHEVROLET DEALER . . . . Race Street
SAM BUTLER, FRUIT MARKET . . . . Race Street
WHITE STAR LAUNDRY, MR. LAWRY . . . . Railroad Street
HO SANG, CHINESE LAUNDRY . . . . Race Street
SAM SAG, CHINESE LAUNDRY . . . . Race Street
W. PORTER, PLUMBER . . . . Race Street
H. KIFER, PLUMBER . . . . Oak Street
C. A. McGUIRE, JUSTICE OF THE PEACE . . . . Race Street
SQUIRE VINCENT J. HOLDEN, JUSTICE
   OF THE PEACE . . . . Race Street

FIREMEN

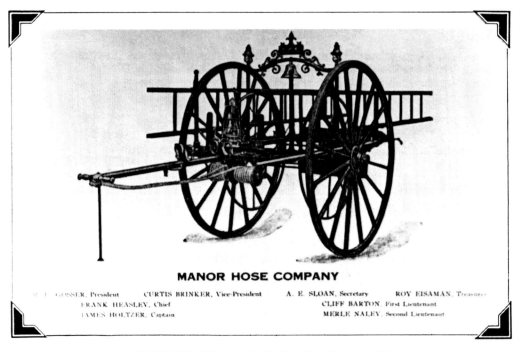

MANOR HOSE COMPANY

W. J. GOSSER, President   CURTIS BRINKER, Vice-President   A. E. SLOAN, Secretary   ROY EISAMAN, Treasurer
FRANK HEASLEY, Chief   CLIFF BARTON, First Lieutenant
JAMES HOLTZER, Captain   MERLE NALEY, Second Lieutenant

HISTORY OF MANOR HOSE COMPANY

The Manor Hose Co., was organized May 29, 1895. The meeting was called to order by John C. Peoples. W. J. Kemerer was appointed Secretary. The following officers were elected.

President — H. S. Struble   Secretary — J. W. Smeltzer
Vice Pres. — John C. Peoples   Treasurer — P. H. Naley

The officers elected having taken charge of the Meeting, they proceeded to organize the Fire Co., to be known as the Manor Station Hose Co. #1, with the following officers:

First Fire Marshal — Frank L. Fry
Foreman   — Jos. Moore
First Ass't.   — W. J. Kemerer
Second Ass't.   — Leander Murphy

MEMBERS

W. F. Brinker	Jos. Crawford	J. L. Flaherty
W. H. Morrow, Jr.	John Hoover	J. P. Wilson
Jos. A. Berger	H. C. Snyder	Sam A. Stauffer
Seth Gosser	C. A. Shirey	Chas. Steiner
J. A. Kemerer	J. F. McWilliams	Grant Keister
Jos. Bigham	Warren C. Fry	S. H. Schmidt
Geo. W. Miller	Bert Suter	H. G. Beamer
Chas. Verner	Jos. Mathias	A. T. Beamer
C. H. Brinker	Robt. McLanahan	D. H. Caldwell
John Baker	A. B. Greenawalt	
H. S. Struble	Howard Hershey	

PLUGS

No. 1	Planing Mill
No. 2	Warren Fry Res.
No. 3	Brinker's Store
No. 4	Naley's Bakery
No. 5	Presbyterian Church
No. 6	Oak and Second Sts.
No. 7	Cleveland and Blaine Sts.
No. 8	Head of Broad St.
No. 9	Oak and Fourth Sts.
No. 10	P.R.R. Station
No. 11	Mathias Distillery

By popular Subscription $86.25 was raised to buy a Fire Bell now in use.

On February 15, 1905, the Hose Co. was re-organized. A box social and dance was held raising $89.50.

From July, 1905 to January 27, 1911, the Hose Co. was in name only and the citizens of Manor in general answered the Fire Alarms.

Re-organization of the Co. January 27, 1911 through generosity of the Council and citizens of Manor and vicinity, we have been able to purchase over eleven hundred dollars worth of apparatus and at present we have in Borough Bldg. one Hose Cart with 550 ft. of hose and some Chemical, Rubber suits etc., in the Hose House on the Hill we have one hose Cart with 500 ft. of hose and also Rubber Suits which you plainly see, gives Manor the best fire protection.

OFFICERS - Names on Picture of Fire Cart

President	M. E. Gosser
Vice. Pres.	Curtis Brinker
Secretary	A. E. Sloan
Treasurer	Roy Eisaman

Chief	Frank Heasley
Captain	James Holtzer
1st Lt.	Cliff Barton
2nd Lt.	Merle Naley

On January 27, 1911, the present Co. was re-organized with the following officers:

President	J. W. Smeltzer
Vice. Pres.	D. H. Crock
Secretary	Roy Eisaman
Treas.	W. J. Kemerer
Chief	F. E. Heasley
Capt.	W. F. Brinker

On September 23, 1911 the Co. held a supper and cleared $339.44 and with an apportion of $300.00 from council the Co. purchased more rubber suits etc.

MANOR FIREMEN AT THE 1914
CONNELLSVILLE CONVENTION

A group of Manor Firemen attending the Firemen's Convention at Connellsville in the year 1914.

The two sitting in the forefront, (left to right): Mike Palmasano and Dick Kellner. The rest of the group in the rear, (left to right): F. R. Heasley, Clair Steiner, Frank Penman, Jim Beamer under the arrow, A. R. Martz, Frank Kooser, Ralph Grieves, William Fisher, Jim Holtzer who is partially hidden, Cliff Barton, Albert Sloan and Clyde McWilliams.

FIRE DEPT. OFFICERS OF 1925

The officers of the Manor Fire Department are, front row (left to right): Bill Stouffer, Ford Heasley, Bill Brinker, Jim Beamer. Back row (left to right): John Elkins, Andy Lomicka, Jim Mellon, Vic Kornrumph, Dick Kellner and Frank Heasley.

Picture courtesy - Virginia Beamer Crum

MANOR FIRE ENGINE 1926

In the drivers seat here is Jim Mellon and under the arrow is Jim Beamer.

Picture courtesy - Virginia Beamer Crum

MANOR FIRE DEPARTMENT — YEAR 1927

A full crew assembled for this picture taken beside the Borough Building. Holding banner left to right: Herb Shotts and Jim Loughner.

First row, (left to right): Jim Beamer, Tom Sproat, McCurry, H. Balsley, Carl Schott, Evans, Sam Heasley, Babe Hoak, Bus Flaherty, Harry McKelvey, F. Heasley, Russ Naley, Frank Cosgrove, C. W. Borland, Bert Cox, W. F. Brinker, Dick Kellner.

Center row, left to right: Frank Kooser, Dave Holmes, M. B. Walker, Alan Beamer without the cap, Lewis Stouffer, Jim Ferguson, Ed Smith, Orion Pinkerton, Vic Kornrumph, Ray Guy, Rich Kellner, Bill Rigney, Jim Mellon, Cliff Barton, Andy Lomicka, Emil Reichert, Sam Butler, Bill Stauffer.

Top row, left to right: Jim Wiser, John Cullen, Tom France, Carl Truxell, Ford Heasley, John Elkins, Bud Heasley, Frank Pink, Clair Hanna Sr., Ed Kellner, A. R. Martz, George Templeton, Vincent Holden Sr., Bill Smith.

ONE HUNDRED YEARS OF FAITHFUL SERVICE
MANOR VOLUNTEER FIRE DEPARTMENT
1895-2005

This documentation updates the history as recorded in the 1990 Centennial Book of Manor. The Fire Department continues to keep busy handling emergencies in the Borough and surrounding communities.

OFFICERS AND MEMBERS OF THE FIRE DEPARTMENT
2005

Pres.	M. Radakovich	**FIRE OFFICERS**	
V. P.	D. Gongaware		
Sec.	C. Depp	**Chief**	H. Yost
Asst. Sec.	M. Horsman	**1st Chief**	G. Stutz
Fin. Sec.	T. Miller	**2nd Asst.Chief**	J. Shoaf
Treas.	A. Horsman	**Captain**	S. Gongaware
Chaplin	V. Mahl	**1st Lt.**	S. Wood
Trustee	R. Gongaware	**2nd Lt.**	J. Dixon
Trustee	T. Yost	**Safety Off.**	Bill Fink
Trustee	T. Morris		

MEMBERS

Scott Allen	Bill Baker	Scott Cox
Bill Davis	Lyda Davis	Cliff Depp
Marianne Hermanson	Terry Dzendzel	Dave Gongaware
John Gongaware	Rob Gongaware	Steve Gongaware
Greg Hensel	Tom Horsmon	Stan Karwoski
Georgann Lippert	Vicky Mahl	Brian Mahl
Tim Miller	Todd Morris	Mike Radakovich
Greg Stutz	Jeff Shoaf	Terry Walter
Aaron Wigfield	Scott Wood	Henry Yost
	Tim Yost	

LIFE MEMBERS

Marty Altenbaugh	Babe Brigode	Fred Depp
Paul Dzendzel	Albert Horsmon	Joe Hurst
Wilbert Jones	Don Nicholson	Joe Radakovich
Jack Sproat	Earl Stewart	Tom Stutz

JUNIOR FIREMEN

Bud Mahl	Tom Lalor	Jacob Hensell

MANOR FIRE DEPARTMENT 2005

Since the publishing of the centennial book in 1990, the Fire Department has been kept busy taking care of emergencies in the Borough and the surrounding communities. We purchased a 1993 Sutphen 1500 G. P. M. Pumper with the generous help of the Borough Council and the citizens of the borough through donations in our Yearly Fund Drive. The effort put forth by our volunteer members each year towards fighting fires, dealing with civic emergencies such as the recent landslide in South Wales, raising funds, working at our Lenten fish fries, etc. to keep the department viable, is really outstanding.

In 2003, with the need to update our rolling stock, we purchased a 2003 Sutphen 1750 G. P. M Pumper with the help of Borough Council. Also purchased were new air masks and uniforms to help the Firemen better protect the Citizens of the borough. Although we fight fires small and large, none was worse than the fire on the Manor-Harrison City Road in 2004 in which a young boy lost his life.

The Fire Department is grateful to the Borough Council, the citizens who have donated money and helped, and all the families of the volunteers who help. In recent times all volunteer agencies have needed more help, and our Fire Department is no different. Due to lack of support the annual Firemen's Labor Day Fair and Parade have been cancelled. We greatly regretted this move.

By Al Horsman

CHURCHES

UNITED METHODIST CHURCH OF MANOR

The Manor Methodist Episcopal Church, as it was then called, began its existence in mid Sept., 1871 with meetings being held every two weeks in the schoolhouse. Our first church building was constructed during the Fall of 1873 and dedicated Nov. 23rd. It was a frame building 30 ft. by 50 ft. with 2 doors in front, a steeple and bell, windows on the sides only, and 3 banks of pews. There was a platform across the entire front, with the pulpit in the middle, the choir on the left and "amen corner" at the right. Heating was by 2 large stoves, one on either side, and lighting was by kerosene lamps. Electric lights were installed about 1903 and a coal furnace provided the heating in 1909. In 1914 other pews were installed, with a central aisle, and the 2 front doors were replaced by a central one.

By 1922 overcrowding required more space, so in mid July construction was begun on the present building and dedication took place Apr. 29, 1923. (During the intervening time services were held in the hall in the old Bank Building.) Our new building was first covered with beautiful stucco which, however, could not stand our climate and was replaced with Inselbric in 1938 and this, in turn, was covered with aluminum siding in 1968. In 1919 the property adjoining the church was purchased for a parsonage, two rooms and bath added and a complete renovation made. In 1941 the garage was built and in 1965 the property across Atlantic Ave. was purchased for an

85

Educational building and parking lot. Through the years much has been done (and still continues) to make improvement in buildings and equipment. Proper buildings and equipment are necessary for performing the Lord's work which, after all, is the only reason for the existence of the church. The salvation of souls, through Christ, and their nurturing in growth and constancy are ours, and the Lord's work.

From the beginning Manor, Penn and Harrison City churches constituted a Charge, with one pastor, except that in the Fall of 1893 the emerging church at Pitcairn replaced Penn for one year. But in the Spring of 1952 we requested a 2-point Charge and Penn was removed (thereafter being served by a part-time minister). Similarly Harrison City was removed in 1960 and we became a Station Charge. On Sept. 12, 1971 we celebrated the 100th anniversary of the founding of the church here - it was a great day!

In early years denominational policy required short pastoral tenure, but we have had 3 long pastorates - by Bracken, McCune and, presently, McAdoo. List of pastors follows:

PASTORS

Wiley W. Roup	Fall 1871 to Spring 1872
Solomon Keebler	Spring 1872 to Spring 1874
Edw. W. Williams	Spring 1874 to Spring 1875
Joseph J. Hays	Spring 1875 to Fall 1876
John Huston	Fall 1876 to Fall 1879
John McCarthy	Fall 1879 to Fall 1881
Andrew J. Ashe	Fall 1881 to Fall 1884
Henry J. Hickman	Fall 1884 to Fall 1886
Barnett T. Thomas	Fall 1886 to Fall 1891
Zenas M. Silbaugh	Fall 1891 to Fall 1894
Samuel J. Laverty	Fall 1894 to Fall 1898
Levi S. Peterson	Fall 1898 to Fall 1899
Charles C. Emerson	Fall 1899 to Fall 1903
William H. Barber	Fall 1903 to May 1907
Walter S. Trosh	May 1907 to Fall 1909
John Bracken	Fall 1909 to Fall 1921
S. O. Dorsey	Fall 1921 to Fall 1923
Harry L. Wissinger	Fall 1923 to Fall 1926
Charles T. Murdock	Fall 1926 to Fall 1928
Harold M. Couchenour	Fall 1928 to June 1932
Frank W. Webb	June 1932 to Fall 1934
William T. Robinson	Fall 1934 to Fall 1935
Joseph Lamy	Fall 1935 to Fall 1939
Alexander Taylor	Fall 1939 to Fall 1940
G. Elmer Schott	Fall 1940 to Fall 1941
Wallace L. Faas	Fall 1941 to Fall 1946
John Cogley	Fall 1946 to Fall 1948
G. Dean Krepps	Fall 1948 to Fall 1949
John G. Strain	Fall 1949 to Fall 1952
Lawrence C. McCune	Fall 1952 to Spring 1960
Larry C. Jewell	Spring 1960 to Spring 1963
Robert L. Critchlow	Spring 1963 to Spring 1966
John C. McAdoo	Spring 1966 to

Picture courtesy - Bethie Cox

METHODIST WOMEN'S GROUP

Back row (left to right): Mrs. Greek, Mrs. Ed Smith, Mrs. Gross, Annie Lauffer, Florence Heasley, Mrs. Berlin, Mrs. Pierce, Mrs. Pritchett, Alva Brown, Mrs. King, Mrs. Yokem, Mrs. Balsley, Berth Steiner, Mrs. Gardner, Mrs. P. H. Naley.

Front row (left to right): Mrs. Anderson, George Heasley, Bethie Cox, Rex Cox, Edie Cope, Brice Heasley, Ruth Heasley, Mrs. Catherine Heasley, baby Catherine Heasley, Edith Heasley, Mrs. Hinemarch, Mrs. Blocker, Mrs. Emerson, Mrs. Heasley Sr., Mrs. Frank Steiner, Mrs. Kate Yinger, Mrs. Lichtenfels.

Picture courtesy - Mrs. Catherine Heasley

MANOR YOUNGSTERS

A group of young people pose for a picture in 1926 by the Methodist Church, with Mrs. Tarbert (wearing hat).

Identified are: Sara Preston, Ruth Pitcairn, Mary Francis Larzelere, Ruth Larzelere, Ruth Stall, Alva Brown, Clyde Berlin, Bobby Aiken, Lorain Steiner, Ruth Heasley, Lillie Rowe, Ivan Preston, Gladys McGee, George Heasley, Ruth Bower, Kenneth Berlin, Pauline Barras, Mable Brown, Jim Preston, Emeline France, Paul Brown, Edith Heasley, Ronnie Elkins, Eva Pfeil, Margaret Clinebell, Edith Lauffer, Helen Bowers, David Bowers, Ida Clinebell, Jean Good, Anna Davis.

COMBINED CHURCHES SUMMER BIBLE SCHOOL AT
PLAYGROUND CC 1990

FIRST UNITED METHODIST CHURCH OF MANOR 2005

PASTORS

John C. McAdoo	Spring 1966	to	June 1978
Leroy L. Hollenbeck	June 1978	to	June 1983
Larry R. Neal	June 1983	to	June 1988
Emily A. Byrd	June 1988	to	June 1992
J. Darlene Willams	June 1992	to	Present

During **1965** and **1966** there was much consideration of a possible merger of two or more churches in Manor. All four churches were invited to participate. The Lutheran Church withdrew early from the discussion and somewhat later the United Church of Christ did likewise. Eventually, congregational votes were taken in the Presbyterian and Methodist churches, but the approval vote was considered insufficient to justify further action.

1974: The Educational building exterior was upgraded. Some interior upgrading was also begun.

The Adult Fellowship Class sponsored the first congregational family weekend in Jumonville. This yearly weekend event continued until 2000.

1975: New kitchen completed in the church; a new piano was purchased for the church social room.

1979: The Allan Digital Computer 301 organ was purchased and dedicated in December.

The church Sanctuary was completely remodeled to match the existing architecture of the church.

A ramp was built to the front of the church and tied to the narthex.

1983: A parcel of land was leased from the Borough at a dollar a year for 99 years.

1985: Completed the Lexan covering of the windows.

Bequest from Mr. Harry Brown established a memorial fund.

The Alva and Harry Brown Memorial Trust Fund helps outreach programs defray cost for youth to a Methodist Church Camp. The Community Bible School also benefits from this fund.

1986: The 'Angel Project' improved the Church Basement.

1987: New Living Praise Hymnals purchased and dedicated in March. New Choir robes were purchased. The Choir performs at the 10:45 service, and does the Easter and Christmas Cantatas.

A tape ministry of all services is now done. New ceiling fans were installed in the sanctuary.

December 1987 Began a Community Sunday School with the Presbyterian Church that continued into the 90's.

1999: Improvements to the interior of the church and a new digital piano was donated by Mrs. Cleo Perry.

2001: The former Percy Barber and Ludwig properties were purchased and razed to construct the new Preston Building. A bequest from Ivan and Lola Preston made this construction possible. The building is a memorial to them. It holds the Preacher's Office and is used for Sunday school, programs, dinners, etc. The church family worked many hours to help construct this beautiful building designed by Architect Jeffrey Schroder.

PRESTON BUILDING 2005

2005: A new Sound System installed and parking lot blacktopped.
Services: Sat. Eve. 7 PM; Sun. 8:30 AM and 10:45

This Church is truly blessed with a continuing Army of God's Saints over the years, giving of themselves immeasurably.

By Loretta Schroder

FIRST UNITED CHURCH OF CHRIST

Prior to 1885 the people of the Reformed Tradition of Protestantism were a part of The Brush Creek Reformed Church.

In 1885 under the guidance of Rev. Henry Keener, The First Reformed Church of Manor was organized with forty-eight charter members. They purchased the triangle of ground of the Humphrey Ludwig farm bordering on Observatory, Butler and Blaine Streets and constructed their church which stands, with additions and alterations, at the same spot today.

During the ministry of Rev. C. L. Noss the building was enlarged and the brick veneer added to the structure.

On June 26, 1934 the church became known as The First Evangelical and Reformed Church because of the merging of two denominations, The Reformed Church of The United States and The Evangelical Synod of North America.

In 1957 the Congregation again had its name changed to the First United Church of Christ when the mother denomination again merged with The Congregational Christian Church and adopted the name of The United Church of Christ.

On February 1, 1959 the Brush Creek-Manor Charge was dissolved so that the two congregations were no longer served by the same pastor but were two independent congregations.

On July 29, 1970 the building was struck by lightning and considerable damage resulted. Restoration was immediately begun and the restored and refinished sanctuary was rededicated on April 4, 1971. Completion of the restoration of the water damage in the basement was carried out at a slower pace and was finally completed in 1975. This final completion was celebrated on July 27, 1975 when the congregation celebrated its 90th Anniversary.

MINISTERS SERVING CONGREGATION

1771-1816	John W. Weber
1819-1879	Nicholas P. Hacke
1885-1886	Henry F. Keener
1887-1894	Albert E. Truxal
1895-1901	Thomas S. Land
1901-1903	Daniel H. Leader
1903-1928	Charles L. Noss
1928-1932	Alton W. Barley
1932-1939	Russel C. Eroh
1939-1944	Henry A. W. Schaeffer
1944-1950	Lloyd Voll
1951-1958	George H. Yoder
1958	G. A. Teske (supply)
1958-1961	Jacob Painter (supply)
1961-1964	James Cameron
1964-1965	Clarence Anderson (supply)
1965-1967	Robert D. Barroll
1967	Raymond C. Strine
1979	Reverend Strine retires
Interim pastor	Reverend J. M. Kim
	Reverend Bash
Pulpit filled by lay or supply ministers	
2001	Reverend Rob. R. Clouser

MEMORIES

The mind holds many memories
Both pleasant and unpleasant as well,
This one is seeking forgiveness
Repentance is the story he tells.

By Enid Walter

The Story Follows...

FIRST UNITED CHURCH OF CHRIST SANCTUARY 1971

Enid Walter relates this story from her church's history
This letter was received:

Pastor,
A very long time ago I did something that is regretted to this day. A young fellow, my senior by one year, and myself started hanging out, running together and getting into trouble. At the time money wasn't easy to get but we both smoked and couldn't get it from our parents because we weren't allowed or even old enough. He belonged to this church and knew where the children's collection was kept. So while I watched he went in and took some change. This happened 2 maybe 3 times. I can't remember but I do remember doing it. The money went for cigarettes and candy. Not knowing how much was taken, but thinking not very much, possibly a few dollars. I'm sending this money with this letter hopefully to right this wrong I've lived with for a very long time. I hope you can find it in your heart to forgive for I am truly sorry for what was done. I also pray that God forgives me also.

- A member of a 12 Step Program

The envelope included $100 cash.

UNITY EVANGELICAL LUTHERAN CHURCH

Unity Evangelical Lutheran Church in Manor had a slow and difficult birth. The beginning of this congregation can be traced back to the Rev. J. S. Fink, who was pastor at Brush Creek from 1868 to 1881. He regularly held services in Manor. While he served as pastor, plans were made to build a church. Unfortunately, a dispute arose as to whether to build the church in Manor or Westmoreland City. When no agreement could be reached, plans were dropped.

In 1886 there was again talk about building a church. At the time the Rev. F. W. Kohler of Irwin was serving the community of Manor. In September of that same year a constitution was adopted and signed by 46 members. For the following year and a half this struggling congregation held services in both the Reformed and Presbyterian Church. Then in 1888 they disbanded for some unexplained reason.

Unity Evangelical Lutheran Church was finally and permanently organized in 1891 under the leadership of the Rev. S. K. Herbster. A constitution was adopted, and a lot on which to build a church was acquired. The church was at last built and the cornerstone placed on February 2, 1902. In November of that year the church was dedicated.

The Rev. Herbster served the congregation until 1910. He was followed by the Rev. E. H. Daugherty, who remained until 1941. During his pastorate an annex to the church was built.

When Unity Lutheran Church celebrated their fiftieth anniversary in 1941, it was noted that Manor is "an over-churched community" and our "growth in membership has been slow." This was borne out in 1974 when Unity yoked with St. John's Lutheran Church in Boquet and called the Rev. Dennis D. Kiesling to be their pastor.

At first Unity Evangelical Lutheran Church belonged to the United Lutheran Church in America. Today Unity is a congregation in the Western Pennsylvania - West Virginia Synod of the Lutheran Church in America.

Pastors who served this congregation from the time of its organization, are as follows:

PASTORS

Rev. S. K. Herbster	1891 to 1910
Rev. E. H. Daugherty	1910 to 1941
Rev. N. G. Fatman	1941 to 1953
Rev. E. N. Kilburn	1954 to 1957
Rev. J. B. Spielman	1958 to 1969
Rev. O. L. Arnal	1970 to 1972
Rev. D. D. Kiesling	1974

UNITY EVANGELICAL LUTHERAN CHURCH OF MANOR
PASTORS

Following Pastor Kiesling was Rev. Donald Power, and then Rev. James Mayer. In October of 1995, we received Pastor Norman E. Nething as our interim pastor. Pastor Nething retired in 2002. We then welcomed Rev. Bruce Brunkhorst as our interim in October of 2002. Rev. Brunkhorst was the pastor for our final worship on September 5th, 2004. The church is now closed.

THE SANCTUARY MURAL WAS DONE BY LUDWIG SCHEUERLE DURING HIS COLLEGE YEARS AS AN ART STUDENT AT CARNEGIE UNIVERSITY.

By Avis Reichert Altman

THE HISTORY OF THE MANOR PRESBYTERIAN CHURCH

The Manor Church was first known as "The Manor Station Presbyterian Church". This Church had its beginning in the Union Sunday School that was held in the town school house during the early seventies. They were encouraged to organize a Church by Ministers by the name of Kane, Ewing and Spargrove who occasionally held services after Sunday School.

At a meeting of Blairsville Presbytery held in the city of Johnstown in January 1875, a petition was received from citizens of Manor and vicinity asking Presbytery to appoint a committee to visit that point and if the way be clear to organize a Church. The request was granted and Ministers Davis, Townsend and Brown together with Elders, McConahey and Hope were appointed. These men soon visited the field, and the way was found clear; the Church was organized on the 24th day of May 1875, with twenty one charter members. At the time of organization James F. Fullerton, John Morrison and J. F. McWilliams were elected, ordained and installed Elders of the Church. W. H. Morrow, H. E. Ludwick and John Loughry were the first Deacons. The Rev. T. F. Boyd, a Minister in the United Presbyterian Church, who had been preaching in Murrysville and Beulah, was the first Minister.

The services of the Church were held in the school house while a building was being planned and erected. The building was completed in 1877. The lot cost $100.00. The stone for the foundation was taken from Brush Creek not far distant and was quarried by the men and boys of the Church. Mr. Isaac Baer, who owned a planing mill, furnished the lumber at cost. Most of the work of erecting the building was donated. The cost of the building was $2,000.00. The Church was dedicated in the Fall of 1877 and the Dedicatory Sermon was preached by Dr. George P. Hays, who at the time was resident of Washington and Jefferson College. This Church served the Congregation for 52 years, but for several years the growing needs of the Congregation necessitated a new and larger building. In 1928 a building program was made and followed which used the old building, but gave the Congregation practically a new Church. This was done at an expenditure of $28,000.00. The new building was dedicated September 23, 1928. A note was given for this amount. But payment was delayed by the depression and the Church did little more than to pay the interest. As times improved there was a renewed interest in the payment of the note. The Board of National Missions was contacted and the note was reduced to $9,000.00. In May 1943 a new movement was started which called for a system of payments to cover 30 months. A Forward Movement Committee was organized with Mr. Ralph Evans as Chairman. Until that time Mr. W. F. Greenawalt had been Secretary of the Building Fund. Mr. Elmer Cullen was named treasurer of the Committee. It was with the cooperation of all the societies and members of the Church that this Committee finished raising the necessary funds and the Mortgage can now be burned.

The following Ministers served as Pastors:

1875 – 1876	Rev. T. F. Boyd
1877 –	Rev. Kirk
1884 – 1888	Rev. Frazier
1888 – 1889	Rev. Jones
1890 –	Rev. J. M. Kelly
1899 – 1907	Rev. Harry Calhoun
1909 – 1914	Rev. J. W. Stewart
1916 – 1921	Rev. T. F. Kerr
1922 – 1925	Rev. H. A. Smith
1926 – 1944	Rev. C. W. Chadwick
May, 1945	Rev. O. Emerson Washburn

Elders in addition to those mentioned at the organization of the Church, the following have served the Congregation, W. F. Greenawalt, J. C. Misel, J. H. Hazlett, Null Suter, E. L. Grabel, Dr. C. P. Snyder, Frank Goodman, John Lewis, W. J. Hanna, George T. Ankeny, W. F. Greenawalt Jr., Bert Cline, E. M. Palmer, P. N. Riley, Robert Stewart, Ralph Evans, Thomas Gaebel and Rex Harden.

UNITED PRESBYTERIAN CHURCH MINISTER 2005

The United Presbyterian Church is fortunate and blessed to have Thomas Holmes as a pastor and spiritual leader. Pastor Tom and his wife are parents of three sons. They reside in Vandergrift.

During WWII, twenty-one young men from this congregation were called or volunteered their services to our country. Of this group, two men made the supreme sacrifice; Vincent Arbaugh, the only child of Mr. and Mrs. Clifford Arbaugh and Edward Hamilton, the only child of Mr. and Mrs. W. D. Hamilton.

In 1975 the One Hundredth Anniversary of the Manor United Presbyterian Church was celebrated. This church still has an active group known as "The Women's Association" that includes all the women of the church. It was organized in 1912.

The church is proud of this group and the many things in which it is involved. Aside from Bible Study and spreading God's Word, there is a Prayer Chain for those in need. Lap robes are sewn, walker bags, and clothing protectors are made for the sick and shut-ins. Donations are made to the Salvation Army, Food Banks, and other Mission Projects. Volunteers also visit Redstone. The women's group meets every Thursday at 10 AM. The men of the church meet on the same day to do the many tasks of maintenance work of the Church.

On a proud note, Jack Sproat, the son of Jack and Betty Sproat, graduated from Waynesburg College and spent three years at Pittsburgh Theological Seminary. He was ordained as a minister on January 17, 1974. While he pastored a church, he continued studying and received his doctorate degree. He is the first member in the history of this Church to become a minister.

MANOR HISTORY MEMORIES
Vivian Horsman tells this story from her youth

Whenever there was a wedding in Manor, we kids would go to the Church and wait outside with pots and pans, and spoons to bang on them. When the wedding couple came outside, we expected them to give us coins. If they did it at church, we would go away and not bother them anymore. If they didn't give us the coins, we would follow them around banging on our pots and pans until they came up with some coins to give us.

SCHOOLS

Picture - John Naley

SANDY HILL SCHOOL

This is the Sandy Hill School, in the early 1900's which was located in Penn Township, north of Manor along the Sandy Hill Road, about 100 yards south of the present entrance to the Norwin Elks Club, on the opposite side of the road.

This school could have been built about the middle of the 1800's. The date on the sign above the windows, is not very clear, but appears to be 1888. Nine grades were taught in this one room school.

This picture was taken during the summer vacation, as can be seen by the lack of ground maintenance. During the school term, the only maintaining of the grounds was performed by the teacher and the pupils. The Sandy Hill School was discontinued in 1925, and was razed a short time after.

"On the diffusion of education amoung the people rests the preservation and perpetuation of our free institutions."

- Danial Webster 1837

MANOR SCHOOL

This picture of the pupils from Manor School was taken in 1895. The school was a wood frame building and at that time consisted of only three grades.

Some of the pupils identified are: Front Row (left to right): 1st Vella Myers, 2nd Martha Smith McElfresh, 3rd Vivian Brinker, 7th Helen Wilson, 8th Joe Mathias, 9th Lilly Rowe, 10th Millie Myers, 11th Blanche Emerson, 12th Florence Naly Rigney.

Second Row (left to right): 1st Margaret Cameron, 5th Charles Lauffer, 8th Curt Gardner, 9th Wilbur Greenawalt, 10th Christ Walthour, 11th Fred McWilliams, 13th Mike Palmasano.

Back Row (left to right): 1st Teacher - Florence McWilliams, 2nd Hazel Kunkle, 3rd Howard King, 5th Will King, last one in back row - Jim Peoples.

CLASS OF MANOR - EARLY 1900's

The two men in rear from (left to right): Mr. Enach, Principal, and George Long, Assistant Principal.

The six girls in rear (left to right): Edna Fry, Ethel Cook, Lucy Stahl, Edith Anderson, Amy Fry, Ida Tallent. Front row (left to right): Arnold Caldwell, Emma Kooser, Henry Beamer, Ruth Suter. Boy in front of Principal Enach, is Alfred Smith.

MANOR SCHOOL 1905 — GRADE 4

Mr. Hetrick, is the teacher at far right in the rear. Fourth row (left to right): Earl Crawford, Jack Caldwell, Blanche Emerson, Henrietta Hershey, Josie Burger, Millie Myers, Margaretta Crock.

Third row (left to right): Pauline Brinker, Jean Errett, Gertrude Altman, Carlyle Caldwell, John Eisaman.

Behind the first row to the left (not in order) Percy Barber, Clair Steiner, Jim Peoples, Roy Eisaman.

Behind the first row to the right (not in order) Gladys Barber, Margaret Wilson, Marie Kunkle, Lillian Stahl.

First row (left to right): Ray Schmidt, Frances Grable, Mary Kooser, Margaret Goodman, Wilson Isett, Guy Blackburn holding the slate, Helen Wilson, Margaret O'Brien, Lee Peoples, Sam Heasley, Fred Brinker, — Crawford.

Photo courtesy - Bethie Cox

FIRST GRADE MANOR SCHOOL ABOUT 1907

Some of the pupils identified are: Adam Bridge, Ruth Beamer, Catherine Brown, Edna McElfresh, Mary Suter, Amelia Palamasano, Mary Burger, Wayne Caldwell, Frances Flacherty, Agnes Galliger, Dude McElfresh, Matilda Galliger, Ida Loughry, Ed Kellner, Bethie Cox, Jane (Beamer) Brown, Ash Crescenzo, Edna Pitcairn, Howard Heasley, Kenneth Eaton.

Picture courtesy - Bethie Cox

MANOR HIGH SCHOOL

The three years of high school taught in Manor at this time were Freshman, Junior and Senior.

This picture was taken shortly after the beginning of the 1916-1917 school term, on the school steps facing Broadway Street.

Identification — front row (left to right): Ester Reese, Sarah Caldwell, Miss Kohl, Alta Baughman, Ruth Beamer, Agnes Gallagher, Bethie Heasley, Edna Pitcairn, Marie Pritchett. Middle row (left to right): Henry Kramer (partially hidden), Wayne Caldwell, Tom Grace, Walter Seigfried, Elmer Thompson, John Naley, Curtis Kooser, David Caldwell. Third row (left to right): Jack Glesenkamp, Edna Cullen, Velma Baughman, Florence Ferguson, Mildred Lemon, Elizabeth Mellon.

Two teachers at the rear (left to right): Principal Leitzel and Miss Glenn.

MANOR GIRLS' GLEE CLUB 1930-1931

Three girls in first row: Sarah Marks, Enid Walter, and Eleanor Lauffer.

MRS. BROWNE'S FIRST GRADE CLASS 1941

Three boys identified: Bobby Sproat, Charles Blank, and Eddie Saddler.

MISS STAHL'S SECOND GRADE CLASS 1948-1949

Front Row (Left to Right): Bob McCurry, Marie Blank, Carol Coffman, Susan Harrison, Bob Davis, Carol Lauffer, and George Walker. Middle Row: Marie Hensell, Charles Altman, Janice Venzon, Virginia McElfresh, Peggy Kline, Keith Brockett, Jack Koebler, and Nina Miller. Back Row: Marlyn Lender, Ruth Reese, Sandra Meyers, Judy Oblak, Ronald Hickman, Theresa Edwards, Marlene Gregor, and Grace Lender.

Picture courtesy - Bethie Cox

MANOR HIGH SCHOOL 1917

Picture courtesy - Mary Ann Walter

MANOR JR. HIGH SCHOOL 1950

Picture courtesy - Phylis Pietrusza-Levino

THE FORMER MANOR SCHOOL 2005

MANOR SCHOOL HISTORY

History records school buildings in Manor in the 1800's as being poorly constructed "one-room shacks, unpainted and un-plastered, cold, barren"... with "rough desks and seats." But the education was always superior. The buildings were either blown down or burned down, located outside of town or on a hill in town, until 1901 when Manor Junior High School was built on the corner of Broadway and Blaine Avenues. For nearly 100 years the school bell rang from the bell tower above the Broadway Avenue entrance, summoning children to school.

Manor School functioned as an independent district until 1950. From the 1920's on, students would attend Manor School for grades 1-10, and then complete their education in a neighboring high school. Students could go to the following high schools: Greensburg, Jeannette, Irwin, Penn Township, or Norwin that later became North Huntington, then was renamed Norwin once again. In 1950, Manor School became part of Hempfield Area School District. Students continued to choose their high school until 1956. At that time, the new Hempfield Area High School for grades 10-12 opened and became the high school for all Manor students.

Several times during the 1980's, the Hempfield Area School Board tried to close Manor School, claiming that the enrollment had dropped. There was a large public outcry, and two times the closing was forestalled. In 1989, when the School Board reported that it would close the school, there was little opposition. Most parents wanted their children to go to a newer school where it was perceived they would get a better education.

MANOR SCHOOL'S LAST FACULTY 1989-1990
Back Row: Ralph Hensell, Paula Boyle, Robin Highland, Ginny Parker, Phylis Pietrusza, Judy Smith, Dominic Gentile, Paula Ostrom, Jo Ellen Numeric, Principal Cheryl Troglio, Front: Helen Hopkinson, Pat Hart, Pat Shirley, Beth Miller Not shown: Music: Gilda Downs, Gym: Keith Cline

When the school building was sold to Chuck Charee, parts of it were remodeled into offices and apartments. The former school now houses a day care center, and the second floor is rented to the Westmoreland Intermediate Unit. The bell was removed from the tower, and can now be seen mounted outside Manor National Bank. The first United States President John Adams said that on the Fourth of July, all bells should ring. What wonderful memories would come to mind at the sound of that old bell - memories of old teachers and of old friends. Some of the "old teachers" I remember when I taught at Manor are Mrs. Malligan, Mrs. Plues, Miss Lessig and Mrs. Sofko. An entire book could be written about the life of Manor School. When the school closed in 1990, the teachers were dispersed to various Hempfield Area schools.

In 1976, during the bicentennial celebration, Principal Norman Pezzi and PTO President, Pat Stawicki were granted approval to paint murals on the walls of the school.

NORMAN PEZZE   PAT STAWICKI

Funds were raised to purchase paint and materials to complete this project. Everyone helped - teachers, staff, parents, and interested citizens joined in the fun. Mrs. Stawicki remembers in particular Lucy Shaffer who worked long into the night on many occasions. Mrs. Shaffer added shadings and lines to bring the murals to life. The project took nearly two years to complete, but when it was finished, there was not a place on the walls of the school that were left unpainted. Today, only several murals remain, but Mrs. Stawicki has retained a photo album of the entire work.

1976 MANOR SCHOOL MURAL SECOND FLOOR

In 1990, Manor's centennial year, the school closed. At this time, the community held a reunion for former teachers and students. There was a special postal cancellation for Manor that year as it celebrated its Centennial and the reunion was a grand event. But the loss of the school has created a void in Manor that remains to this day.

By Phylis Pietrusza-Levino

FOUR GENERATIONS OF MANOR SCHOOL PUPILS

Appropriately posed at the entrance of Manor School are four generations in a family line that epitomizes the traditions created in a small community, and the continuity of family. Elizabeth "Bethie" Heasley Cox, her daughter, Audrey Cox Kozain, Audrey's son, Raymond Jay Kozain and Jay's two children, Dana and Andy, are pictured here.

Bethie Heasley's family moved to Manor when she was three years old. Her mother, Florence Heasley, taught school in Manor. At a later date, Florence served on the school board. Bethie attended Manor School for 11 years. She graduated in 1918. Audrey was a student at Manor for ten years and completed her last two years at Jeannette High School. Audrey's son, Jay Kozain, was also a student at Manor and finished his last four years of high school at Hempfield. Jay's children, like all Manor students of that era, moved on to complete their education at a Hempfield school. They were students at West Hempfield Jr. High School until the family moved to Batesville, Mississippi.

When talking with people who come back to their old hometown, one is often amazed to learn of the ties to the school. The Heasley, Cox, and Kozain families are examples of these ties and of devotion to the community in which they lived. Audrey Cox Kozain still lives in Manor on Cleveland Avenue.

By Audrey Cox Kozain

MR. GUIDO J. CICCARELLI
TEACHER, PRINCIPAL, FRIEND

Mr. Ciccarelli is one teacher former students of Manor Jr. High School should remember well. He was born on September 12, 1921 in Monessen and attended California State Teachers College, known today as California University of Pennsylvania. He graduated in May 1947. One month after graduation he married his wife Emily. Soon thereafter he was hired by Lester Kleckner to teach Industrial Arts, Science and Biology in the upper classes at Manor.

MANOR SCHOOL FACULTY 1947

He states that from the beginning he could see that Manor was a nice small town. The size of his classes was also small. In 1947 there were 50 students total from seventh grade through tenth grade. He remembers having only 17 students in his first tenth grade biology class, some of whom he remembers by name. He recalled first the names of the four girls: Lorena Kline, Betty Jean Anthony, Jean Gongaware, and Eloise Altman. The boys were a little harder to remember. From this class, he recalled: Warren Bietel, Bill Roscher, Ronald Baughman, David Gosser, Tommy Altman, Paul Haubrich, Sam Schroder, LaVerne Bush, Dale Allison, and Walter Kotok.

HOME ROOM CLASS 1947-1948

Recalling names of former students was not difficult after the school started producing yearbooks. Prior to 1949 there were no yearbooks in Manor School. Yearbook companies didn't want to make books for schools with small classes. The students made the first yearbook at Manor School in 1949. Eddie Barton did the artwork. In trying to remember names of his first students Mr. Ciccarelli said he had a picture in his head of the seating arrangement.

Sometimes teachers quickly remember the students that gave them the most trouble, but that is not the case here. Mr. Ciccarelli fondly remembers how nice the kids were. He didn't have discipline problems. The students were all very cooperative. He remembers one cold winter day getting stuck in the snow after school. He had a long drive to Monessen and needed help getting his car on the road. His students hauled ashes from the boiler room in the basement of the school to give his car some traction and to help him on his way. Young people today wouldn't know about ashes and coal furnaces.

CLASS OF 1951

For the first three years he taught at Manor, Mr. Ciccarelli and his wife lived in Monessen. Then in 1950 they moved into an apartment on the second floor of the home of Hazel and Holly McCurry at the corner of Blaine and Cleveland Avenue. He moved into a new home he built on Sandy Hill Road in 1954.

The jointure with Hempfield in 1951 dramatically changed the class size in Manor School. Hempfield had an abundance of students but no space. Manor had space but few students. The arrival of students from these schools caused a number jump from 17 per class to 30.

From the seventh through the tenth grades the student population increased to over 200. The students came from Wegley, Penn, Adamsburg, and High Park. The first year was difficult for everyone. Manor students were not happy about the invasion, and the new arrivals were not happy to be there. The kids formed cliques and stuck together. While discipline had not become what teachers today call a problem, Mr. Ciccarelli said the teachers then "had to watch more carefully." However, watching more carefully wasn't a challenge because of the good faculty. The teachers worked together. Support was steadfast, and the paddle was still in use. At a recent all-class reunion the master of ceremonies asked those people paddled by Mr. Ciccarelli to stand. He said every person in the hall stood, including the women. He laughed. He said he never spanked a girl and certainly not that many boys.

In 1954 Guido Ciccarelli was made principal of Manor School. He compliments the teachers he worked with and remembers them with high regard. There was Annabelle Kleckner who taught English, Jim Rutledge taught geography and history. Later, Fred Pellegrene replaced Mr. Rutledge and Roberta Silvis was hired to teach Geography. Mr. Amada Yocabush taught music in the room beneath his biology room. Mr. Ciccarelli said to this day he has yet to forget the song *Jada*. Helen Bossart taught Home Economics and Loughery Wegley taught Health. Mr. Wegley was also in charge of athletics. Later Ted Kondrad replaced him and Ruth Brace replaced Mrs. Bossart. When Mr. Ciccarelli first came to Manor School in 1947 he was surprised to learn he would be teaching with two of his old classmates from California State, Wilfred and Helen Hepler. The Heplers were equally surprised and pleased. They were the first Manor residents to invite the Ciccarellis for a social visit in their home.

In 1966 Mr. Ciccarelli left Manor School to become principal of West Hempfield . In 1970, he was made Assistant Superintendent of Hempfield Schools. He held the position of Acting Superintendent of the District in 1978 and again in 1983.

He says that the years he spent at Manor were some of the best years of his life. He is now 84 years old. He and his wife Emily still live in their home on Sandy Hill Road.

By Guido Ciccarelli as told to Gail Martz Noll

"I remember Chick coming to school the day Rosemary was born. He was so excited he told us all he couldn't have gotten dressed without little Wayne's help. Wayne chose his father's tie and made sure everything matched!"

- Helen Hopkinson, colleague

Manor School reunion: relia

By DEBBIE KONDEL
Lifestyle Editor

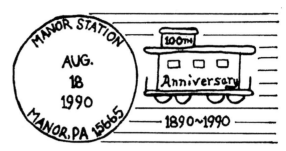

A group of Manor area residents gathered Thursday night to say goodbye to the old and at the same time mark the beginning of a new century for the borough.

Over 200 people attended the Manor School Reunion to mark the closing of the 89-year-old structure and recapture a few old memories. Former and present students, teachers, PTA members, and administrators gathered in the gymnasium of the facility to say goodbye to a structure that has served as the focal point of the community for so long. They walked the halls of the two-story building still filled with the sounds of school from so long ago.

The Manor Elementary School, now part of the Hempfield Area School District, will be closed at the end of this school year. Built in 1901, the building was a junior high school until 1966 when it was changed to an elementary school.

Decorated in blue and white, the school colors, the gym was the focal point for the celebration. Items and photos from each decade of the school's life span lined the perimeter of the room. A majorette uniform from the 1960's and yearbooks emblazoned with the bulldog, the school's mascot when it was a junior high, were exhibited. A class photo from 1919, yellowed with age, depicted the graduating class with its seven members. A banner recognized the 1948 Westmoreland County Basketball Champions from Manor.

Many of the items were put on display by former students. A display by Elizabeth Heasley Cox showed four generations of her family had gone through the school. Mrs. Cox herself attended the school for eight years, from 1908-1919.

Betty Jane Frye Graham went to the reunion because she attended the school in the class of 1931-32. A Manor resident all her life, her son also graduated from Manor. Now her nine-year old granddaughter, Michelle Lynn, goes there.

In 1917 John Naley was 17-years-old and a junior at Manor. The 90-year-old pointed out his position in the class photo along with that of his wife, Florence Ferguson Naley, then a senior. "This (the gymnasium) wasn't here then," Naley added.

Paul Dzendzel looked over a group of paintings hanging in the second floor hallway. Spotting one titled "Subway," he stopped his wife, Jean, and friends, and says, "There it is. That's it." Dzendzel was one of four students who painted the scene for an art project in the 1943-44 school year. He joined Dale Bush, Fritz Horsmon, and John McKissock in creating the scene that would become a part of the school's decor for years. "The 'subway' was the farthest point outside we could go from the school to do it," Dzendzel said. "I don't even remember what part I did. Maybe that little building." The teacher for the project was Mary Glunt.

Joanne Parkhurst was one of the people who "got the ball rolling for the reunion." Three generations of her family have attended the school.

"It was really very selfish on my part, because I wanted to see everyone again," she explained. She was overwhelmed at the number of people attending the event. "It was all by word of mouth." Individuals from throughout Manor donated the cookies and the students at the school made paper flowers for the teachers and dignitaries.

Lester and Annabell Kleckner also attended the reunion. Mrs. Kleckner taught seventh, eighth, and ninth grade English at Manor for several years. She left in 1945 to go to West Hempfield.

Her husband was principal at Manor for 10 years, from 1945 through 1955.

The Kleckner's were greeted by one of Mrs. Kleckner's former students, Karen Dygan, herself now a teacher. Dygan said, "Every day I get up in the classroom I just pretend I'm her (Mrs. Kleckner). She taught, directed the class play, and did everything."

Also attending the reunion was Guido Ciccarelli, a former assistant superintendent in the Hempfield Area School District. Ciccarelli, who retired seven years ago, began his career in education at Manor. The former Monesson resident started as a teacher at Manor, teaching everything from biology to industrial arts. "In those days, you taught everything," he added.

He became a principal in 1954 and in 1966 was principal at West Hempfield. He was appointed to the position of assistant superintendent in 1970.

In conjunction with the reunion, the borough's Centennial celebration was officially opened. Centennial planners are still working to prepare the 100-year history of the school, the Centennial logo was displayed on hats and T-shirts. The logo, in the form of a postmark, depicts an "anniversary" train (1890-1990) moving into Manor Station.

As the crowds toured the school building, many stopped to tug on the rope, ringing the old school bell which over the years warned hundreds of students school was about to start. Many guests at the reunion also marveled over the murals painted in 1976 to give life to the school for the country's bicentennial.

ing 89 years of memories

Manor reunion

Over 200 people attended a reunion at Manor Elementary School this week to mark its closing at the end of this school year. Those attending gathered in the gymnasium (top photo) to exchange stories and memories of school days in the 89 year old building. One of those reliving memories was Paul Dzendzel (right photo) who was one of the artists who created the painting behind him entitled "Subway." Dzendzel, along with Dale Bush, Fritz Horsmon and John McKissock completed the painting for an art project during the 1943-44 school year when Manor was a junior high school. The painting, along with several others, decorate the second floor hallway of the elementary school. (Standard Observer photos)

Correction to Observer Photo - Pictured above: Fritz Horsmon

SPORTS

BASEBALL

The first record of baseball in Manor was kept in 1874. Manor fielded a team that year and for the next ten years was very active.

The members of this team were: James Slotter - 3rd baseman; Blayer Matron - left field; J. G. Kennedy - short stop; Steve Naley - pitcher; Emery Naley - 2nd baseman; Rush Marchand - center fielder; Warren Fry - 1st baseman; W. F. Brinker - catcher and Captain, with R. H. Miller - right field.

Other members of the team were: the Welty boys, Dave Miller, Harry Taylor, Will Taylor, Will Heintzelman and Jacob Best.

Their opponents were local clubs which included Adamsburg, Arona, Irwin, Greensburg, and others.

Two members of this team later operated businesses in Manor; W. F. Brinker owned a hardware store on Race Street and Emery Naley was a carpenter and contractor who became involved in building quite a few houses in Manor in the early 1900's.

In 1900-1903 Manor again became prominent in baseball, claiming the championship of Western Pennsylvania. A team from Arona was a strong contender in these years and was always stiff competition for the Manor team.

This team played together for many years and was recorded as playing the Pittsburgh Pirates at Manor when "Old Honus Wagner" was Pittsburgh's Star Short-stop. Members of this team in these years were: W. F. Brinker - Manager, Cremer - catcher, Stotler - pitcher, Martland - short-stop, Reynolds - first base, Jordan - second base, Stewart - third base, Hart - left field, McKechnie - Middle field, and Steiner - right field. Charlie Steiner remained a resident of Manor, through most of the 20th century.

Independent baseball became very popular in this first quarter of the 20th century in Manor and the surrounding towns including Irwin, Jeannette, Greensburg, Scottdale, Pitcairn, Wilmerding, Turtle Creek, East Pittsburgh and others.

Several leagues were in operation during this period, two of them being the West Penn League and the Inter-County League. Manor was a member of both of these leagues during their operation. The Manor field had a large grandstand between home plate and third base, and later bleachers were built between home plate and first base. These two stands were nearly always filled, and many watched from along the left field line which was adjacent to Kemerer-Moore planing mill. Also, many sat or stood on the hillside across Brush Creek, which was the Mathias and Whitehead property.

There were travelling ball teams during this period and many times one or the other would visit Manor. They included the "House of David" team; the Homestead Grays; the Donkey team; and the Bloomer Girls.

Baseball reached its peak in Manor early in the 20th century when the Homestead Grays visited Manor. This Homestead team was owned, coached, and managed by a prominent Homestead citizen by the name of Cum Posey. His whole life was baseball, as his team would start playing early in the spring and continue until fall. Some of those playing on the Manor team during this time were: Mike Palmisino, Horsmon, Zeke King, John Stanko, Bill King, Sam Heasley, John Fry, Campbell, Ben Robinson, Simon Whitehead, Bert Keller, Yellow Keller, Red Hurley, Homer Goodman, Bunny Goodman, and Merle Naley.

These Homestead Grays were all strickly big league material and had Oscar Owens, a pitcher who could have pitched in the major leagues. He had two catchers who worked with him, George Gibson and Washington.

The team king, Oscar Owens had a style all his own. He and his teammates injected a lot of comedy in their style of baseball. Years later in basketball, another good team known as the Harlem Globetrotters used comedy to highlight their games.

When a batter, came to the plate, Oscar Owens, would stare at him for a few seconds, circle around the pitcher's box a few times, and then occasionally would walk to the batter's box and talk to the batter. There was no time limit on pitches in those days, with the pitcher having time to do his act. Sometimes before he pitched the first ball to a batter, he would walk out to second base and wave all the outfielders in, so they were close to first, second, and third base. He would then casually walk to the pitcher's mound and proceed to strike out the batter. Such was the style of Oscar Owens and the Homestead Grays, who were usually unbeatable.

Later other leagues were formed in which Manor fielded a team; namely the Keystone league and the News-Dispatch league. A Church league was organized and all the churches in Manor participated. Later the baseball interest was confined by the American Legion teams.

With the coming of better transportation such as the railroad, the street cars, and the auto, this great interest in independent sports waned.

A story, taken from the History of Baseball in Manor and written by Joe Pike is shown below.

Picture - John Naley

BASEBALL STYLE 1878-1884

Standing left to right: James Slotter-3rd base; Blayer Matron-left field; J. G. Kennedy-short stop. Steve Naley-pitcher; Emory Naley-2nd base; Rush Marchand-center field. Sitting left to right: Warren Fry-1st base; W. F. Brinker-catcher; and R. H. Miller-right field.

Baseball

Date 1878-1884

I recall a game that was pulled off between Manor and Penn whenever Will Heintzelman was Captain of the Manor Club. This game was played at Manor, and the Penn Club won by a score of 6 to 2. Heintzelman was indignant, and in his positive way of putting things; he challenged the visiting club to play another nine innings; alleging that only a part of his club had been represented in the first game. A second game was then played which resulted in a score of 1 to 0 in favor of Manor.

During this time there were some swift games being played between Adamsburg and Greensburg. One in particular of which I recall was staged at Adamsburg. There was threatening weather during the forenoon with frequent light showers of rain, but the visiting club showed up in good time and took dinner at the Shotts Hotel, and beside having dinner, the highballs being called for by some of the fans were shared by some of the players. About one o'clock word had been sent out that the game was to be played "rain or shine".

However, all the baseball players now realize that you cannot mix highballs with curve balls or low balls and also become a star at this profession.

Amidst jangling, this game had been interrupted a half dozen times, and free for all fights were indulged in which not only ball bats were used freely, but guns were pulled and some shots were fired. Some of the players and spectators as well, saw the closing innings of that game

---

with one eye closed. My old friend, W. H. Altman, of near Manor was a spectator at this game and did much to restore order and keep the peace. Manor played a game at Greensburg on the last Saturday of June, 1884. Train #18 carried the team to Greensburg, this train due to leave Manor at 1:54 P.M. and on arrival at Greensburg, we were met and were taken to the Fisher House where we took dinner, and from there we secured a photographer and had the team's picture taken and then were taken to the Fair Grounds. After a few preliminaries the game was begun and lasted only one hour and five minutes, and resulted in a score of 2 to 4 in favor of Greensburg. The shortness of the game may be attributed chiefly to the fact that foul tips if caught put the batter out and base runners also if the ball could be played before the runners returned. It was not uncommon to see triple plays made in that way, starting with a foul if caught.

J. G. Kennedy, played short for Manor the first four innings of this game and threw out 6 men at first base and caught two flies, only of which was legally mine as it was a rule with our club—that no two men would ever attempt to field the same fly balls, but everything seemed to be coming my way. As this second flyball was batted so high that it deceived everybody and I presumed, of course, that since I had started to field it that all the others had left it up to me to finish. After backing up a considerable distance, I was forced to turn my back to the batter and run as only a Dutchman can. I arrived there just in time to clinch it, and the first realization that I had that others were trying to field this fly ball was whenever the feet of our second baseman, Emory Naley, went flying past my head. Whenever we came out of that conclamoration, there was James Slotter, third baseman, and Blayer Matron, left field; all were after the same fly ball. Captain Brinker censured us severly but each pleaded ignorance of any knowledge of anyone else after that ball. I excused myself to our captain by telling him that I intended going Railroading the first of the month, and was familiarizing myself with the highball in advance.

Here, I want to make reference to the excellent work of this club. Steve Naley, as a pitcher had a peculiar way of holding the ball, always squeezing his thumb into the palm of his hand, and using chiefly his two forefingers. I had never known him to play out or even to tire out and he often pitched 12 or 14 innings. Warren Fry, Emory Naley, and James Slotter always played the bases and had no fears in their day when it came to filling these positions. Blayer Mattron, Rush Marchand, and R. H. Miller always played the outfield and no uneasiness was ever felt by the members of the club when it came to throwing out a runner at home plate. Brinker was captain and catcher on this club, and he was known to be "Honey" by name and by nature.

We returned to Manor on the train known as the Uniontown, due at Manor at 5:22 P.M. thus being absent from Manor less than 3 hours and 30 minutes. On arrival at Manor, the first persons to greet us were our old friends: W. H. Morrow, Jin Portcher, Pete Naley, and Peter Whitehead; each smoking Andy Ramsey stogies made expressly for the Dutch. They tried to console us but said that it had been predicted that we were to get a thrashing.

BUT ECH MOX NIVOUS.
Sincerely yours,
(Signed) Joe Pike

103

BASEBALL – 1903

This picture of a Manor Baseball team, was recorded as having been taken in 1903, in Homestead, Pa.

This team held the Championship for an independent team for awhile in this vicinity.

Players shown here are, top row (left to right), first not identified, second Porter. Middle row (left and right), Charley Steiner, William Brinker, Cosgrove, McKeckney. Bottom row (left to right), first not identified, second Stotler, third not identified, Jordan, and Ed Cramer.

EARLY 1900's BASEBALL TEAM

This was a good Manor Baseball Team that played in the early 1900's, when it was at the pinnacle of popularity.

Picture taken in deep center field at Manor Ball Park.

Identification, front row (left to right): Harry Brown, Dude Barton, Sam Heasley, Zeke King. Middle row (left to right): Unknown, Bert Keller, Homer Heasley, Melms, Ray Kreuzberger, Mike Palamasano. Back row (left to right): Marsh Horsmon, Unknown, Ralph Grieve, Bill Stauffer, Bunny Goodman, Merle Naley, Sol Wilson.

MANOR ATHLETIC CLUB TEAM

This baseball team known as the Manor A. C. played in the early 1900's.

Sitting (left to right): Yellow Keller, Zeke King, Mike Palamasano Chal Barton. Standing (left to right): first two unknown, Adam Helbig in black suit, Roy Eisaman, Homer Heasley and Spike (Howard) Walthour. The boy not identified.

BASEBALL — THE BEGINNING OF THE 1900's

This team represented Manor in the early 1900's and were a formidable opponent of the Homestead Grays.

Back row, (left to right): Homer Heasley, John Eisaman, Bunny Goodman, Manager Sloan, Bill King, Chal Barton, and Roy Eisaman. The boy in picture is Manager Sloan's son Bud.

Sitting are, (left to right): Yellow Keller, Zeke King, Mike Palamasano, Lindsey, Bert Keller.

BASEBALL IN THE 1920's

This Manor baseball team played in both the West Penn League, and the Inter-County League. These leagues included local teams such as Irwin, Jeannette, Grapeville, Pitcairn, Wilmerding, Turtle Creek, Scottdale and others.

Players shown here are back row (left to right): Red Hurley, Goodman, Marsh Horsmon, Bunny Goodman, Larry Rankin the Manager, Dude (Ray) Barton, Ben Robinson, John Fry and John Stanko. Middle row (left to right): Russel Guy and Harry Brown. Bottom row (left to right): Ray Kruesberger, Hunt, Zeke King, Lindsey, Sam Heasley and Bert Keller.

BASEBALL IN 1943

The Carl Leroy McKelvey Post 472 sponsored a team in the American Legion League. The team was sponsored from 1943 to 1993, for 50 consecutive years! The Pennsylvania American Legion gave a plaque to the Post for this outstanding achievement.

BASKETBALL EARLY 1900's

Independent basketball had a decade or more of popularity in Manor in the early 1900's.

This team played in the H. A. Lauffer Auditorium, which was on the second floor of the Lauffer store, later the store of J. R. Sowash, and today is known as the Manor Market of Paul Lehman.

They played local teams, such as Irwin, Jeannette, Pitcairn, Turtle Creek, Wilmerding and a few Pittsburgh teams. The big attractions were usually played on Christmas Eve or New Year's Eve.

Three of the Pittsburgh teams they played were, the Coffee Club, located in Oakland, the Lafayette Big Five from downtown Pittsburgh, and the Second Storry Morrys, located on lower Fifth Avenue in Pittsburgh. The name, Second Storry Morrys was given to the team by their sponsor, a Men's Clothing Merchant, whose slogan was 'Walk up one flight of steps and save half', hence the name "Second Storry Morrys". Al Abrams, sports writer for the Post Gazette, still talks and writes about the Second Storry Morrys.

The players in this picture are, front row (left to right): Adam Helbig, Roy Eisaman holding the ball dated 1908-1909, and Charley Whitehead.

Rear row (left to right): John Eisaman, Bunny Goodman, Bill King, Chal Barton and Zeke King.

MANOR FOOTBALL TEAM AT BOLIVAR

Manor played Bolivar, at the Bolivar Athletic Field, which was located next to the Pennsylvania Railroad. Manor was victorious in this game. Bolivar and Donora were regularly scheduled and tough opponents of the Manor team.

Identification here, front row (left to right); Russ Shotts, Sam Godfrey, Stan Eaton, Carl Truxal, Odin Douglass. Middle row (left to right): Frank Kooser, Melms, Bob Wilson, Marsh Horsmon. Back row (left to right): John Emerson, the coach, Herb Shotts, Ralph (Gin) Grieves, in the gray jersey a member of the Bolivar team, Tom France, Bert Keller, Clair Steiner and Sam Heasley.

The player in the gray jersey was a member of the Bolivar team, and a long time friend of Tom France. He wanted to have his picture taken with the Manor squad, which he considered a very good football team.

MANOR FOOTBALL TEAM EARLY 1900's

This squad was coached by John Emerson, who had coached other football teams in the early 1900's.

The location of this field is not known. The identification of players are, front row sitting (left to right): Ben Long, Clair Steiner, Sam Heasley, George Grieve, Carl Truxal. Center row (left to right): Harry Brown, Mun Higgins, Tom Sproat. Back row (left to right): John Emerson, (the coach), Hank Davis, Carl Grieve, Ralph Grieve, Unknown, Tom France, Bert Keller, Frank Kooser and Mike Palamasano in the Manor jacket.

"There is an intensity and a danger in football - as in life generally - which keeps us alive and awake. It is a test of our awareness and ability. Like so much life, it presents us with the choice of responding either with fear or with action and clarity."

- John Brodie

Picture courtesy - Stan Eaton

FOOTBALL TEAM READY TO TRAVEL

This group, members of the Manor Football Team of 1910 to 1914, were ready to travel to Bolivar, where they were scheduled to play this day. At this time, most of the traveling was by commuter trains.

Identification of this group, kneeling (left to right): John Emerson, and the Coach Sam Heasley. First row standing (left to right): Sam Godfry, Melms, Odin Douglass, Bob Wilson, Carl Truxal, Stan Eaton, Frank Kooser, Carl Leroy McKelvey. Back row standing (left to right): Fin Keller, Ralph (Gin) Grieves, Clair Steiner, Herb Shotts, Marsh Horsmon who is partially covered, Bert Keller, Russ Shotts.

About three years after this picture was taken World War I was in progress and Carl McKelvey shown here, was one of the early casualties. The Manor American Legion Post was named in honor of him.

MANOR SCHOLASTICS FOOTBALL

The Manor Scholastics Football team played in the early 1900's, and their opponents were local teams from, Larimer, Hufftown, Mount Pleasant, Scottdale, Latrobe, Bradenville, Loyalhanna and Herminie #2.

The game that the Manor people and the team looked forward to was the one with Herminie #2. This game was usually played at the end of the season, and at the opponent's field. The coal company at Herminie sponsored this team, and one of the mine officials whose name was Cargo, was their manager and coach.

The game was played on a field overlooking Herminie next to the coal mine.

The team used the miners' shower building to suit up, and change clothes after the game.

A banquet was held immediately thereafter, in one of the hotels located on the main street of Herminie. The Manor team was the only team to get this special treatment.

Identification in this picture, rear row (left to right): Stan Eaton Manager, Assistant Coach and player, Curt Kooser, Bill Sofko, George Davis, Wayne Caldwell, Ellis Hockenberry, Fred Horsmon and Coach Charley Borland. Coach Borland was a graduate of the University of West Virginia, and played as a teammate of the great Ira Rogers.

Second row (left to right): Russ Fulmer, Tom Grace, Miles (Fats) Berlin, Glenn Parry.

Bottom row (left to right): Francis (Bus) Flaherty, Jack Glesenkamp, Carl Truxal, Harry McKelvey, Charles Beatty and John (Tuck) Flaherty.

Courtesy - Bethie Cox

FOOTBALL TEAM – 1917

Independent Football was popular at this time, and shown here is one of the Manor teams of that era.

Front row (left to right): Dick Taylor, Tom Grace, John Kooser, Williams, Vic Tilbrook, Babe Hoak.

Second row (left to right): John Flacherty, John King, John Kemerer, Bill Rigney, Carl Truxal, Ike Scheuerle.

Back row (left to right): Curt Kooser, Jack Glesenkamp, Jud Meek, Eugene Rankin, Bert Cox.

MANOR FOOTBALL TEAM 1920 - 1924

This football team played mostly local teams, Irwin, Jeannette, Larimer, Trafford Indians, Pitcairn Mohawks, Herminie No. 2, Mount Pleasant, Hufftown, Loyalhanna and Bradenville.

When the team traveled, some went by train and others by automobile.

Identification here, front row, (left to right): Tom Grace, Harry McKelvey, Charles Beatty, Carl Truxal, Glenn Parry, Ellis Hockenberry. Middle row, (left to right): Russ Guy, Miles (Fats) Berlin, Bert Cox, Bus Flaherty, Jack Glesenkamp, Curt Kooser. Back row, (left to right): Russ Fulmer, manager Bill Sofko, Ralph Orr, Russ Beamer, Stan Eaton, assistant coach Wayne Caldwell, Fred Horsmon, John Havel and Mr. Charles Borland head coach.

TRAIN WRECKS

Courtesy - The Lawsons

WRECK ON MANOR VALLEY BRANCH
OF THE PRR – YEAR 1900

This wreck occurred near the northern end of Race Street on the Manor Valley Branch, close to the Freedom Oil Co. building. This oil and petroleum center was served by a siding which lead from the PRR Manor Valley Branch. An oil tank car is shown on this siding, near the wreckage. The open fields and orchard behind the smoke is part of the Walthour farm.

Picture courtesy - Mary Ann Walter

THE OVERHEAD BRIDGE BEFORE 1980 TRAIN WRECK

UNIONTOWN EXPRESS
WRECKED – MAIN STREET
CROSSING, MANOR

Three members of the crew and a signalman at the tower were painfully injured in this wreck, though none were hurt seriously, they were taken to the hospital for treatment. None of the passengers were injured beyond slight scratches from flying glass – Sen. John M. Jamison was in the smoking car but aside from a shaking up was none the worse for the experience.

The engine did not leave the track but mail and baggage cars were smashed to pieces and the westbound tracks blocked traffic for some time. The wreck occurred about 8:30 when one pullman coach left the rails but remained right side up with a number of Greensburgers on the train.

Manor, Nov. 30, 1909. - Uniontown Express train No. 101, westbound, with Conductor Sam Miller in charge, was wrecked here this morning at 8:30 and four men injured: Their names are:

C. F. Steffy, 30 years old, married and lives on Second Street; signalman, ankle broke and dislocated, cut about head; taken to his home.

George M. Scott, 47 years old, married and lives at Fairchance; mail clerk, contusions of the body but not serious; taken to Westmoreland Hospital.

W. E. Quigg, 27 years old, married, home at Fairchance; baggage master, contusions of the body and lacerations of the face; not serious; taken to Westmoreland Hospital.

Harry Kreator, 28 years old, single, home at Altoona; left leg broken; taken to hospital.

SLIGHTLY INJURED

H. M. Pradee of Fairchance, passenger brakeman, riding to Pittsburgh; left leg badly injured.

Miss Alfreda Cook, of Jeannette, suffering from shock. Was enroute to Braddock where she was employed.

W. M. Charles of Greensburg, injured about face and head by flying glass.

Adolph Herskovitz of Uniontown, suffering from shock.

A. R. Klippelt of Fairchance, left knee badly wrenched.

Signalman C. F. Steffy, was in his signal tower at the bridge just west of the crossing when the wreckage swept the tower and its occupant away with it. Willing hands soon extricated him from his perilous position and he was given medical attention.

Express Messenger George, was in the mail and express car with George Scott, but fortunately escaped unscratched. He fell across a pile of mail pouches and was not hurt.

Passengers in the smoking and day coaches were shaken up but no one was injured beyond a few slight scratches from flying glass. One of the excited passengers crawled out thru a broken window when the cars finally came to a stop, and cut his hands by the ragged edges of glass in the window frame.

The train was a few minutes behind time and was sweeping around the curve at Main Street at a high rate of speed. Just as the engine cleared the crossing, the trucks on the baggage car left the track. Immediately the engineer applied the air brakes and the train buckled under the awful strain. The engine and pullman stayed on the tracks, but the heavy baggage, and mail cars, along with four coaches jammed together with such force that the impact completely severed the baggage car into two sections. One was splintered into many pieces, the other section was partially intact resting on the rails and ties. The mail car went part way over an embankment and hung there, a complete wreck.

The only part of the huge engine that left the tracks was the front trucks on the tender, and it came to a stop about 300 yards from the Main Street crossing.

The four passenger coaches were jammed up against one another in a zig zag way, but outside of broken glass and being off the rails, were not badly damaged. The big Pullman coach left the rails but stood on the ties intact. The Uniontown Express left Uniontown Tuesday morning at 6:22 and was a few minutes late when it arrived in Greensburg. Conductor Sam Miller was in charge of the train and the following crew; Engineer McGinnis, Fireman Kennedy and Brakemen Holy and Kreator.

The cause of the train jumping is not known but it is thought that the iron trucks on the baggage car left the tracks near the street crossing. After the wreck, a broken rail was found at the point where the car wheels hit the ties.

The baggage car, which was next to the engine, and in front of the mail and baggage car, pulled the latter car from the rails, broke the couplings connecting it with the tender and rolled down the five-foot declivity into a ditch beside the track. As these cars went down from the track they crashed into the signal tower and knocked it down. Signalman Steffy's leg was broken when he was thrown to the ground in the wrecked tower.

Baggagemaster Quigg, who was in the baggage car at the time, did not have time to jump and was carried with the wreckage into the ditch and received his injuries when the mail and baggage car fell on the baggage car. When the two cars went over the bank and landed in the ditch, both were practically telescoped. The railway mail clerk who was sorting mail at the time, was caught as the car went from the track. The other four cars, the three passenger coaches and the Pullman parlor car, which was the last car on the train, jumped off the rails and stretched across the tracks, tying up traffic.

Rescue work was started at once to get the imprisoned men from within the two cars lying in the ditch. Scott was found lying beneath a pile of mail bags, held down by parts of the wrecked car, while baggagemaster Quigg was penned up in a corner of his wrecked car surrounded by broken wood and trunks.

Physicians from Pittsburgh, Manor, Jeannette and other points along the main line of the Pennsylvania were rushed to the scene of the wreck and gave medical aid to the injured.

Among the Greensburg passengers on the wrecked train were the following: Senator Jamison, Morris W. Head, Miss Rachel Kettering, Mrs. John Latta, Miss Margaret Latta, Mrs. Curtis H. Gregg and Paul Feightner.

Some of the Greensburgers proceeded to Pittsburgh, while others returned home to recover from bad cases of "nerves".

DEVIL'S BEND TRAIN WRECK ABOUT 1910

A Fast Express left the rails at a straight stretch of tracks, about 75 yards east of the dangerous Devil's Bend, and came to rest at the edge of Brush Creek. No reason was given for the wreck.

The lead engine left the rails and pulled the front baggage and express cars down the snow covered embankment.

The express cars were loaded with race horses, most of which were killed outright, and the rest so severely injured, they had to be destroyed on the spot.

All were buried across Brush Creek in the pasturefield of the Becker farm.

Railroad derricks working at the top of the picture show a drop of about 60 feet down to Brush Creek.

THE OVERHEAD BRIDGE LIES ON TRAIN TRACKS FROM DERAILMENT AS VIEWED FROM SOUTH RAILROAD STREET

TRAIN WRECK AT RACE STREET AND DAVE CROCK'S STORE

On March 24th, 1912 at 7:30 P.M., Fast Freight No. PG3, westbound on No. 3 track, came to a screeching halt at the Grade Crossing on Race Street. The train was traveling west at 55 miles per hour, when an axle broke on an oil car, piling up 12 cars in a heap. Interlocking switches by the crossing were all ripped out, and a car swung in back of the small Newsstand Building and hit the end of Dave Crock's Grocery Store. Dave Crock was slightly injured. Manor Firemen were called to the scene, but there was no outbreak of fire. Four wreck trains were called to the scene, two from the Pitcairn Yard and two from the Derry Yard. The cleanup continued all night and all the next day.

During one of the heavy lifts being made, one of the derricks from Derry toppled over and killed one man. At this period of time, the interlocking switches were located near the crossing and further east. The control tower namely M. F. was located close by the building which is now the Manor Borough Hall. There are three separate views of this wreck, each taken from a different angle. The one view shows the small Newsstand, the end of the Dave Crock Store and home, and the railroad people repairing the track.

A locomotive is parked on the Manor Valley Branch Line. The station platform extended out along the line with a fence at the side. A pair of steps, at the end of the platform exited to the rear of the big white building in the background which was the J. R. Sowash Store. At the far rear center is the red brick home on the Walthour Farm. The cleanup and repair of the railroad bed was still in progress.

(Continued on next page)

Another view shows the cars, some of which were broken in half, piled up in a heap, with some of the railroad people surveying the scene.

Another shows the damage to the Manor Valley Branch Line, the Station Platform, and also to the small passenger waiting room.

This view of the Manor Valley Branch Line shows how the track curved around in back of Race Street and followed Bushy Run Creek up the Valley to Harrison City, Clark's Crossing and Claridge.

Pictures courtesy - Bethie Cox

TRAIN WRECK IN 1936

Courtesy - Mr. Frank Pink

The last big train wreck in Manor was in the early morning hours of Friday, March 27, 1936 during a heavy rainstorm and it involved a westbound freight and a "double-headed" fast night express going east. Being guided by the road signal tower, the freight was slowing down as it rounded the curve entering Manor just east of the station. During this slowdown, some of the cars buckled causing a freight car to protrude into the path of the speeding eastbound passenger train, the Philadelphia Night Express. This Express left Pittsburgh around 11:35 P.M. and was travelling about 65 miles per hour, when it sideswiped the freight and within seconds, cars from both trains were scattered over a quarter mile area like toys. A box car was tossed into the side of a dining car; and a mail car was thrown onto the Jeannette-Manor Road, blocking not only the highway but the interurban tracks of the West Penn streetcars. The four-track main line of the Pennsylvania Railroad was a pile of twisted rails and broken ties disrupting service for many hours. As the first locomotive upset, it swept the lines of the West Penn Power substation located nearby and thus the entire town was in darkness. The headlight of a trolley furnished the only illumination for the first rescuers as they helped the crews and some of the passengers sleeping in the coaches from the wreckage. The boilers of the heavy engines exploded as they sprawled over the area and down the embankment from the track. Many ambulances, the Manor Volunteer Fire Department, along with several doctors, hurried to the scene to offer assistance. When all 78 passengers and crew from the two trains were accounted for, the only casualities were three killed and two injured. It was really a miracle that more lives were not lost. Trainmen believed a faulty rail was the cause of the wreck.

WESTINGHOUSE CHEMICAL PRODUCTS PLANT

This is a view of the Westinghouse Chemical Products plant, located along the Manor Valley Railroad.

The plant was originally an independent corporation, secured by the Westinghouse Electric Corporation in 1937, where it was operated as a wholly owned subsidiary until December 1946, when it merged with the parent company as part of the Micarta Division.

The original equipment was an older variety used by the paint and varnish industry of the 30's which consisted of open kettlecooking, of dying oils and hard resins to make varnishes.

Modern methods, using high temperature closed reactors, equipped for distillation and removal of by-products, produces todays synthetic resins.

This plant was modernized in 1948, and later expanded in 1956. It is now part of the Insulating Materials Division, with headquarters in West Mifflin, Pa.

The employes represent a cross section of production, engineering, and administrative skills. Most live in Manor and surrounding communities.

Data and picture, courtesy of Westinghouse Electric Corp.

STORIES OF

MANOR

THEN AND NOW

Painting by George Y. Heasley

MANOR STATION

2005

THE GOVERNMENT OF THE BOROUGH OF MANOR
LAW ENFORCEMENT

The government of the Borough of Manor was enacted in 1890 as recorded in the Borough Council Records of Ordinances, Laws, and Meeting Minutes. These books are held in the Borough Municipal Building and are accessible to the public.

MANOR BOROUGH BUILDING 2005

Most of the history recorded here of the men who were appointed to enforce the laws and ordinances of the Borough of Manor are taken from those documents. However, in this research we have found that some records conflict, especially dates, and there are several omissions. As it often happens in the case of history, the word of those still living is relied upon, trusting that names, dates, and stories move forward with objectivity. Thus, the history that follows is an account of several of the men who were in positions of firsts and lasts and is recorded with respect for the dedication of all men who faithfully served the community.

LAW ENFORCEMENT THEN...

On the second day of February in 1891 the Town Council of Manor Borough enacted into law twenty-one ordinances that were to govern the lives and activities of the residents of Manor in the early years. To enforce these laws, men dedicated to serving and protecting the community were appointed to bring justice to those who broke laws. Joseph H. Burger was Manor's Burgess in 1891. Mr. Frank McElfresh was appointed in 1903 as the first named "police chief" and prior to 1920, Alva Ray Martz was acting constable.

In the Manor community it was common for generations of families to carry on the work of their forefathers. This was true not only for families in business, merchandising, medicine, and banking, but also of government. Four generations of the A. R. Martz Family have been public servants in law enforcement. His two sons and a grandson were police officers in Manor between 1946 and the 1970's. One of his great-grandsons is presently on the Penn Township Police Force.

Some of the men who served as Burgesses in Manor from 1928 to 1946 were H. C. Caldwell, W. H. Stauffer, Z. N. Burger, E. E. Naley, and George Grieve. Constables were few, but those mentioned included Joe Young, William Smith, and John Elkins. When a constable had yet to be appointed, the Burgess carried out those duties in addition to his own. George Grieve found himself in this position on occasions. In 1961 the title Burgess was changed to Mayor.

On May 3, 1946, Burgess C. W. Barton swore in Leonard J. Martz and James Gilchrist as interim deputy constables. William R. Thompson, was appointed to the position of Justice of the Peace.

At the June 7, 1948 meeting, the Manor Borough Council agreed to purchase a police uniform for Leonard Martz, thus making him the first uniformed part-time police officer in Manor.

While the monetary rewards for law enforcement work in Manor were limited, so was criminal activity. An example of such activity in 1909 was partying on Sunday. Borough records show that four men from the "...Jimtown Blocks..." W. R. THOMPSON

were arrested for having a "...dance and jubilee..." on Sunday. Law enforcement problems were of a similar nature throughout the 40's and 50's. They could be labeled vagrancy, disorderly conduct, pranks, drunkenness, peepers, and bums. Very few lawbreakers had to spend a night in jail. During the tenure of A. R. Martz, the jail was the family garage. Later, the jail consisted of a single cell with a cot and toilet located in the Fire Hall near the truck garage.

At the January 18, 1958 Council meeting, Burgess Vincent J. Holden recommended that Wilbert J. Jones be employed as an additional part-time police officer and that Leonard Martz be appointed Police Chief, a position he held until he retired in 1974.

After a meeting of the town council on February 14, 1964, borough police were notified that they were no longer to use their own cars for police duty. The town purchased a used "Police Pursuit Car" from Central Service Station in Jeannette. The car cost $1,500, and that amount was borrowed from the Manor National Bank. The car was delivered in March of 1964, and a garage to keep it in was rented for $3.50 a month. The Manor Police were now visible. They had a car, but still had deficiencies. The protection was still part-time and there was no police station. Manor was growing. The Mount Manor development and the annexation and growth of the Lord Fox Estates resulted in the need for more complete police coverage.

CHIEF L. J. MARTZ

LAW ENFORCEMENT NOW...

On January 3, 1973, Manor Borough Council hired Russel Cain to be the borough's first full-time police officer. One year later, December 11, 1974, Joseph Brucker was promoted to the position of Chief of Police. Then in 1975, there was discussion about the future of the Police Department. The issue was whether or not to continue supporting a full-time/part-time force, or to merge with North Huntingdon. It was suggested to pursue the matter and "bring the information back to the people." This issue was tabled at the August 3, 1975 meeting. There are no records to show how far this idea went. There is only evidence to support that the law enforcement in Manor has remained in Borough control from 1891 to 2005.

In 1978 the second police car was purchased, and one year later Council adopted a police pension plan. In 1981 radio service was switched to 911. David Hanko was Chief of Police. In 1984 a public works building/ police station was completed. This facility is located on the Brush Creek Road across from the ball field.

PUBLIC WORKS BUILDING AND POLICE OFFICE

Because of financial problems in 1986, the Council requested that full-time police officers be terminated and the force be reduced to two part-time men. In 1990 several citizens and business owners requested council establish a six-man police force with around the clock protection. Thus, four more officers were hired part-time to make a total of two full-time and four part-time officers. Two years later Chris Painter was promoted to Chief of Police.

On June 8, 1994, Council agreed to provide police protection 24 hours a day, 7 days a week. In October 1995, the first Teamster Police Contract was signed. In 1997, another full-time officer was hired under a federal grant program which brought the total of full-time officers to three and part-time officers to four. Law enforcement is controlled today by seven men and the town owns three police cars. In the month of March 2002,

George Valmassoni was promoted to Chief of Police. He has this to say about his tenure as a law enforcement officer: "I have worked in law enforcement since 1989 and was hired in Manor Borough in 1991. I have always liked my job. This has been possible due to great support through the years by Borough Council and the mayors past and present. What makes me most proud of being Chief of the Manor Police Department is the great officers I have been able to work with for many years. We are very fortunate to have such a professional, well-trained group of officers serving Manor

CHIEF GEORGE VALMASSONI

Borough. A Police Department is only as good as the men who serve in it."

POLICE OFFICERS 2005
Left to Right: *Patrick Bowman, Christopher Wilson, Elias Hanna, George Valmassoni, Chief; John Johnson, David Romagnoli, Not pictured, David Meyers*

Governing Manor is much the same as it was a century ago, but more people are needed to do the job for a growing community. The first office in the Manor Borough building is the one of the Secretary/Treasurer, Tom Costellic. This office handles all the business and accounting for the Borough.

TOM COSTELLIC

Having experience as a controller of a large company before taking a government job gave Mr. Costellic invaluable experience. A phone call to the Borough building will probably be answered by him.

MICHAEL RADAKOVICH

The other person you will find in the Borough offices is Michael Radakovich. He is the elected tax collector for Manor. He also collects the school taxes.

ED ANTONUCCI   BILL FERRARO

Borough Attorney, Bill Ferraro, attends public meetings, and handles legal matters for the Borough.

Borough Engineer, Ed Antonucci, attends most public meetings and answers questions for the public. He does all the background work for maintenance, investigations for development, and advises the work crew.

All of these people help the elected officers make the necessary decisions that get the Borough business done.

JEREMY FAIT AND
BOB STEVENS
WORK CREW

MAYOR RUTH WILLIAMS

Ruth Williams is serving her second term as Mayor of Manor. She attends Council meetings and reports to Council on the activities of the police department. The Mayor's chief concern is the operation of the Manor Police Department.

MANOR COUNCIL MEMBERS

Back Row L to R: Bob Eathorne, Dave Gongaware, President, Dave Sturgess, Chuck Konkus, Front Row L to R: Mike Kochasic, V.P., and Russ Gadagno. Not Pictured: Rick Poholsky.

The elected Council Members are responsible for running the government of the Borough of Manor. With the advice of their consultants, they make the decisions for the citizens such as was made at the August meeting to allow a new development with approval for 26 new houses.

For one hundred and fourteen years, generations of men and women in this railroad community, known as Manor, have tirelessly given of their time and energy to supporting their community. They perform the duties of corporate officers, governing and preserving the dignity and safety of its citizens, and upholding its constitution and laws. This history is dedicated to the memory of those who have gone before, to those who serve now, and for future generations to preserve and respect.

By Gail Noll, George Valmassoni, and Phylis Pietrusza-Levino

UNITED STATES POSTAL SERVICE
MANOR, PA 15665
P. O. BOX 9998

Phone: 724-863-2152
Postmaster: Karyl Nicholas

Window Hours: Monday – Friday 8:00 AM – 4:30 PM
Closed Noon – 1:00 PM Daily
Saturday – 9:00 AM – 12:00 Noon

The First Manor Station post office was established in 1856, located at the corner of Race Street and Harrison Avenue. The first postmaster was Jim McWilliams.

STATE SENATOR, ALLEN KUKOVICH ADMINISTERS THE POSTMASTER'S OATH OF OFFICE TO KARYL NICHOLAS, MANOR POST OFFICE 1996

When President Cleveland was elected, Mr. Brinker replaced the Republican Postmaster. Later the post office relocated to the building across the street from the Library on Race Street. The post office then moved to the old Manor National Bank Building. At that time, James Beamer was Postmaster. When the Manor National Bank Building was demolished, the post office was temporarily placed in the building where Dvorsky's Costume Shop is now located.

The present Manor Post Office building located at 9 Atlantic Avenue was dedicated to public service in 1968 with Wayne Anthony as Postmaster. Since that time there have been a number of postmasters, including Donald Campbell, Geraldine Foley, Verna Bernard, and Karyl Nicholas who is the present Postmaster.

Picture courtesy – 1965 Tribune Review Article

SITE FOR NEW POST OFFICE

The post office currently employs five people: The Postmaster, Karyl Nicholas, part-time Flexible Clerks, Donna Roberts and Malika Jones Rural Carrier, Cindy Bush, and Contract Custodian, Diane Blawas Thomas.

Mail is distributed daily to 704 post office boxes. The Rural Route travels 14.25 miles per day delivering mail to approximately 450 customers. Mail is dispatched at the end of each day to the Greensburg Mail Processing Center.

UNITED STATES POSTAL FACTS

- The U. S. Postal Service does not receive tax dollars for operating expenses. Revenue from sales of postage-related products pay these expenses.
- When fuel costs raise one cent, our costs increase $8 million.
- Sales of the Breast Cancer Research semi-postal stamp raised more than $42.6 million from nearly 600 million stamps sold.
- Sales of the Heroes semi-postal stamp raised more than $10.5 million to assist families of emergency relief personnel killed or permanently disabled in the line of duty on 9/11/01.
- The "Have You Seen Me" detached direct mail card program that was co-sponsored by ADVO, an advertising organization, contributed to the safe recovery of 136 missing children.

By Karyl Nicholas, Manor Postmaster

THE ANNEXATION

In June of 1957 Charles D. Whitehead, Samuel E. Heasley, and others circulated a petition to Manor Borough Council to annex 1042.19 acres from Penn Township. This petition was signed by 80% of the freeholders in the area to be annexed. The annexation area extended out Sandy Hill Road to and including the Norwin Elks and out Route # 993 to and including the Jerry Nedley property. Manor Borough Council, James C. Gilchrist, President, John L. Naley, Secretary, and Joseph R. Young, Burgess, enacted and ordained the annexation ordinance on June 13, 1957. After prolonged litigation, Judge David H. Weiss of the Court of Quarter Sessions of Westmoreland County approved the annexation by order of court dated February 7, 1963. The annexed area is governed by Manor Borough, however the school district remained in Penn-Trafford. Manor Borough was represented by Christ C. Walthour, Jr. Esq. and S. Wayne Whitehead, Esq. Penn Township appealed to the Pennsylvania Supreme Court, which by decision dated November 12, 1963, affirmed Judge Weiss's order for the annexation.

By Wayne Whitehead

ORCHARD DRIVE   MANOR VIEW ESTATES

When the annexation was approved, Mount Manor development had already begun. The story of Sandy Hill Road relates how the annexation and growth has affected this area. Development continues on the road between Manor and Harrison City (SR993). Looking up Orchard Drive in the picture at left, you can see some of the houses that now fill the large pasture that was on the top of that hill. Further out SR993, another development consists mainly of townhouses. Council recently approved another new development of 23 new houses.

By Phylis Pietrusza-Levino

SANDY HILL ROAD

According to the 1867 Pomeroy Atlas of Westmoreland County, Penn Township Map on Page 51, the property on the eastern side of Sandy Hill Road was owned by Sam Walthour and Dr. J. I. Marchand. It appears that the "old Eaton log cabin" area belonged to J. Kuhns. Beyond that was Marchand's. The old Suhan Mansion belonged to a Mrs. Marchand whose farm continued out to the Harrison City Road. The plaque above the front door dates the house to 1829.

SUHAN HOMESTEAD

Sandy Hill School House No. II sat where the Angelo Pezze home is now. The road appears to run to the west of its present route. Near the school Mr. R McWilliams lived.

The old Mellon Farm, which is now Laffoon's, belonged to J. Naly. The land where Rescue 6 and the Anthony Farm is now located, belonged to a Mrs. Campbell. The land on the western side, of the road lies in North Huntingdon Township.

As years went by more homes were built. James and Margaret Walthour purchased land from the Marchands, and sometime after 1876 they built the farm where the Wergins now live. A house was erected next to the S. Walthour home on the Manor side. Several houses were built near the Eaton Log cabin. On the western side, were the Mellon and Bergman Farms.

OLD WERGIN FARM HOUSE 2005

J. G. Fletcher, a wealthy New York lawyer, married a girl related to the Marchands and turned their place into his summer home. Many old timers remember the caretaker Danny Saylor, as a familiar sight going into Manor everyday in his truck with his big dogs riding in the back.

THE FLETCHER ESTATE IS NOW NORWIN ELKS

Beyond the summer home, the Marchand daughters, Rebecca and Yoland, built a small but picturesque home that is now the property of the Ignatz family.

Next was the farm of Charles Rau that John Yeager now owns. Beyond that, the Suhan home was on the east and the Anthony farm on the west.

Sandy Hill Road was a dirt road until the late 1930's. The WPA put down a macadam road using stone that they got from an old stone quarry on the Wergin farm.

When the Pennsylvania Turnpike was extended from the Irwin exit to the Ohio Line, sand for the concrete was taken from the area where the New England Village now stands and the area between the Parker property and the Pittsburgh Brass Plants. Originally, this sand led to the naming of Sandy Hill Road.

In the 1950's everything began to change. Private homes began to spring up along the road. The snow fences came down. Sandy Hill Road had a great penchant for snow drifting. The "Big Snow of 1950" really had us snowed in. But the new homes were a windbreak.

When Lord Fox Estates was built, it ended picking blue berries or riding horses there. In the 1960's Manor Borough annexed a large area of Penn Township where most of Sandy Hill was located. Most of the residents signed a petition, primarily because we were assured we would get city water which was desperately needed. The annexation went through with the stipulation that the children would still attend Penn Township Schools. The annexed area went out as far, and included, the Fletcher Estate. Manor Borough now ends at Norwin Elks.

CAMERON DRIVE

In the 1950's the Nike Site was constructed on the Mellon Farm. This was during "The Cold War." We could sometimes see the missile launchers rise. It was frightening because we were so close to possible targets. In the 1960's J. G. Fletcher died.

His estate was purchased by a group of Greensburg doctors who in turn sold it to the Norwin Elks. In the 1970's a large housing development called Sandy Hill Highlands was built on a large section of land purchased from the Elks. Cameron Drive is part of that development.

The Sandywood development is now across from the Elks and is still expanding.

SANDYWOOD SITE

Recently Lord Fox Estates became known as New England Village. The area from New England Village down Sandy Hill Road is now populated by private homes and a large housing plan that begins on Fairview Drive, just east of Sandy Hill Road. This plan now connects with the roads in New England Village, the former Lord Fox Estates.

There are several homes on Sandy Hill Road between this plan and the two story red brick house that was built in the 1700's. In 1976 this home was owned by Charlie and Alice Davis. Alice was on the Manor Bicentennial Committee and was instrumental in having the Manor Book published. This house still stands and is the oldest house in Manor.

FAIRVIEW DRIVE

THE DAVIS HOUSE 2005

I must say that the statement that the only constant is change could not apply more than it does to Sandy Hill Road. No more quiet country road, no more chicken coops, no cows grazing, and even worse, no more knowing everyone! It's all changed.

By Cel Wergin. Cel and her husband Chuck live in a new home on the former Wergin farm on Sandy Hill Road.

"Those of you who remember Alice Davis are lucky. Wasn't she a fine person with whom you could spend your time? Her kitchen and a cup of coffee there eased the problems of the day."

- Phylis Pietrusza-Levino

This stanza from *"A Home Song"* surely speaks of Alice.

But every house where Love abides,
And Friendship is a guest,
Is surely home, and home-sweet-home:
For there the heart can rest.

Henry Van Dyke

A LOOK AT SOME OF THE OLDER MANOR HOMES

At the Corner of N. Railroad Street and Broadway stands this red brick house which was the former home of Mr. and Mrs. Hiram Altman and Mr. and Mrs. Chalmers Barton.

At the Corner of Broadway and Atlantic Avenues stands the former home of the Christ Walthour Family, and Evelyn and Chuck Landsperger. Cindy Stennett now owns it.

From this home on Oak Street you can see in the distance off to the right the new Orchard Drive development. This house was once owned by the Kornrumph Family and later by Ethel and Ray Bowman. It is now owned by David and Roberta (Oblak) Franklin.

This house was the home of H. A. Lauffer who was once the owner of the Sowash Store. Later it was the home of Wanda and Jim Klingensmith. It is now owned by Marc and Tracey (Davis) Alaia.

Mr. DeWalt built this brick home, on the corner of Blaine Ave. and Butler Street, after moving the previous home he built there up one lot. This house became the home of Howard and Margaret (Kooser) Lauffer. Later it was owned by Art and Sue (Lauffer) Steffey. It is now owned by Mr. and Mrs. John Stapf.

This was the home of Mr. and Mrs. Zeff Burger. Later Mr. and Mrs. George Greguric owned it. It is located at the corner of Observatory Street and Blaine Avenue.

Located at the top of Broadway and Third Street is the girlhood home of Mildred (Millie) Lichtenfels Tarbert. It was built in the late 1800's.

BREEZE HILL

Picture courtesy – George Y. Heasley

This picture taken from a 1935 post card shows a view looking in a northerly direction from Manor. From left to right are houses along the new Manor-Harrison City Road. The first house was occupied by the Emory Rowe family; the second, the Smith family; the third, the Oscar Felmlee family; and on the far right, McKerracher family. Also, on the right, is the corner of the Kavran barn with the farm and field in the background.

The old red-dog road to the left of the Felmlee house, wound up and around the hill to a place called Breeze Hill, later to be called the Heasleys-On-The-Hill. This Manor landmark was built in the 1800's. Mr. B. M. Yinger purchased this fruit farm from the Crum family in 1911. There were over 300 fruit trees on the farm. With its rolling hills, fertile soil, and good weather, the entire countryside in the vicinity of Manor was noted for the growing of fruit.

After Samuel E. Heasley married Catherine Yinger, he bought the farm from her father. The Yingers and the Heasleys shared the double house where the Heasleys raised four children. The old road at the left bottom of the picture shows the original road between Manor and Harrison City. The wheel tracks road up through the field was changed to a better road in 1946 and the red-dog road was eliminated. Samuel Heasley and his two sons, George and Brice, and some of their friends constructed this road by hauling rock from the farm's stone quarry. Today the road to the farm is called Breezy Hill Lane.

By George Y. Heasley

"SOUTH WALES" OR SOUTH MANOR

When Manor was originally settled it was bordered on three sides by the Brush Creek. The area on the South Side of the Creek was called South Wales. It was called that because most of the coal miners who lived there had come from Wales and Scotland. Most of the first homes were along what is now known as Brush Street, which extended up one block to Penn Street. South Wales was annexed into Manor Borough on February 19, 1921. Some of the families that lived there when I was growing up were the: Roschers, Stutzes, Bosics, Terbots, Oblaks, Kramers, Dvorskys, Pfeils, McKissocks, Campagnas, Washeks, Bobans, Millers, Grabowskis, Holdens, Holmes, Szaramas, Scotts and Clinebells.

The streets in South Wales were dirt streets until the late 1930's when Penn Street was paved from the distillery up to Harding Street. A large distillery was at the bottom of Penn Street. The whiskey was known as *Old Manor*. Mr. Frye and Mr. Mathias were the owners. They owned the business for many years. During World War II this distillery produced pure alcohol for bombsights, alcohol that was used inside torpedos for submarines and medical alcohol. My mother, Olive Jarvis Horsmon, is seen with her mother in the picture above which was taken about 1910.
My mother, Olive, reared me and my brother Fritz here. This house is still there today. Mother was working at the distillery when she died of a cerebral hemorrhage. She wanted to do something for the country because I was in the service. She said, "My son is in the service fighting for the

country and I want to do something to help". She was not a *Rosie the Riviter*, she was *Olive the Alcohol Maker.*

MISS LUCY STAHL'S THIRD GRADE CLASS 1935-1936

In this third grade Manor School class you can find Al Horsmon as the last boy on the right holding the sign. He can point out: Slug Thompson, the Walter twins, Peggy Reichert, Maizie Grieve, and Carl Beretta.

By Al Horsmon. Today Al and Vivian Horsmon live on top of Observatory Street in Mount Manor.

BUSTER'S MANOR NEWSSTAND

Buster's story and a picture of the store is carried in the 1990 Centennial Book, but some highlights and the closing of the store are covered here. That book tells that Buster was then semi-retired but his niece, Linda, and sister Marie, were helping to keep the store open.

LINDA, BUSTER, AND MARIE BEHIND THE COUNTER

When Homer Kifer became postmaster in 1934, he sold his newsstand to Buster who was then just 17 years old. Buster dropped out of high school to devote full time to the business. Several years later he purchased the Dorothy Wilson property.

The United States was engaged in WWII. Buster was drafted in 1942. His mother managed the store in his absence. "It was a challenging experience, but she, with our family, was equal to the task. We had gone through the Great Depression and now World War II added more difficult years. The business was kept together for Buster's return. Delivering the newspapers was traditionally a boy's job, but Mother had to hire girls as paper carriers. During the war years, it became increasingly difficult to stock the shelves, but ALWAYS, penny candy was one on the list," relates sister, Enid.

When Buster returned from the service he wanted to renovate, so he moved into the vacant Jim Lomicka building next door. When renovations were completed he moved back again. The business remained in this spot until it closed on December 31, 1992.

BUSTER WALTER AT THE AGE OF 20 WAS ALREADY A
SUCCESSFUL BUSINESSMAN

Through the years there were occasions when Buster had to guide a
mischievous child onto the *straight and narrow path*. Many a grandparent
learned that they weren't the only reason their grandchildren wanted to
visit Manor. As soon as children arrived, they wanted to be off to Buster's
with their pennies in their hands.

Many memories are recalled, some are funny and some are sad. One
elderly lady who was unable to get *out and about* would call our home
around 4:00 AM and request some one to bring her ice cream and
crackers. This apparently was her regular diet, as she purchased it quite
often. However her days and nights were mixed up, and she would say,
"The door will be open—just bring it in."

This memory gives a feeling of accomplishment. When Buster retired,
Jim 'Sweetmilk' Lauffer wrote to him. He recalled the confidence gained
from the age of ten up through his teen years working for Buster. This
confidence helped lead to his success in the financial business. He states,
"You were an important part of many young people's lives and I am sure
it is part of where each of them are today. Thank you for giving me the
opportunity to learn responsibility and integrity at a very young age." Jim
Lauffer, retired president of the First National Bank of Herminie.

Another memory is of a former resident returning for his mother's
funeral. When he tried to take his children to Buster's Penny Candy Store,
he was disappointed to find it gone. Many people asked Buster to reopen.

BUSTER 1992
When Marian Gardner contacted television station KDKA-TV, Dave Crawley
came to Manor and made a video of the last week of Buster's business.

By Enid Walter.

SITE OF BUSTER'S STORE 2005
IT IS THE THIRD BUILDING ON THE RIGHT.
MILLIE TARBERT LIVES IN THE FIRST FLOOR APARTMENT
TODAY

ED'S ESSO

In 1954 Edward Oblak purchased the gas station on Race Street from Stan Eaton who had been operating it as a Sunoco Station. Following the purchase, it became known as Ed's Esso. This building is now Mort Chiropractic, which also houses a sport gym. Edward and Kathleen Oblak worked many hours pumping gasoline and servicing cars. The Esso brand of gasoline and oil products made some transitions during the 32 years the Oblaks ran the station. Esso became "Humble Oil" for a short period, and then became the well-known "Exxon" brand. For the 32 years that the Oblaks ran the gasoline business it was operated as a full service station. This meant not only dispensing the gasoline, but also cleaning the windshield, checking the oil and checking the tire pressures if the customer requested that service.

In 1960 Ed expanded his business interests into the residential trash business by purchasing a one-truck operation from Charlie Auckerman. Ed later added collection vehicles and containers. He expanded into the commercial business. In 1970 he purchased a roll-off container truck and entered the industrial sector of waste hauling. The era of lower cost per gallon self serve stations led to lower volumes of gasoline being pumped at Ed's. The gasoline business was shut down in 1986. In 1989 the trash business was sold to a public waste company establishing itself in the area, Mid-American Waste Systems.

Many transitions in the waste business during the next 20 years lead to Mid-American being purchased by USA Waste Services. They later merged into the company now called Waste Management Systems. This company is now almost nationwide.

Submitted by William 'Bill' Oblak, now of Clarksburg WV

MANOR COFFEE SHOPPE

THE HISTORY OF RED'S GAS STATION & RESTAURANT

1956 Harry McElfresh built the restaurant. The first tenant was Gordon Holderbaum. It was a soft ice cream and sandwich shop.

1958 Harry built the gas station. It had two pumps, one for regular and one for high test gas. The service was limited to just gas and quarts of oil.

1960 Bob and Genevieve Watson rented the restaurant and started Watson's Restaurant. They ran the restaurant for about 8 years.

1969 Harry McElfresh sold the property to Thomas Stone. It was called Stoney's Gas & Go. Tom added two more pumps. Tom Stone also ran the restaurant for several years selling Chili, Bean Soup, and sandwiches.

1975 Several short-term tenants operated the restaurant.

1981 Tom Stone sold the property to William and Ruby Nesbitt and Theresa Harbaugh. They operated the gas station and opened the restaurant now known as Manor Coffee Shoppe. They sold meals and desserts.

1987 The gas station was closed, then torn down.

1990 William Nesbitt tore down the old restaurant and built the restaurant with a coffee shoppe room and dining room.

2000 William & Ruby Nesbitt and Theresa Harbaugh sold the restaurant to Christine and Bob DeMarchi of Penn Township.

Areas that once were the gas station are now part of the parking lot. It dominates the corner at Sandy Hill Road and State Route 993.

By Virginia McElfresh Wahl

2005 Gary Blank is the new owner, and the new name is: Manor Diner "Home of the Blue Plate Special."

THE MANOR FUNERAL HOME

Around 1918, a period in history prior to the advent of the funeral home, Eli Kistler, a mortician from Harrison City, provided funeral services for Manor residents. Mr. Kistler embalmed bodies at his Harrison City mortuary then returned them to the family residence for viewing. He used J. R. Sowash's seven-passenger Packard for trips to the cemetery. The cemeteries were almost exclusively church cemeteries such as Denmark Manor in Penn Township, Brush Creek, and St. Boniface on Brush Creek Road. The Union Cemetery in Irwin was also a favorite burial place even though it was not church related. Sara Morrow Welty, in her recollections of life in Manor, remembers the first resident mortician being Mr. William Snyder who lived on the south side of the tracks near Peg and Lucy Bair.

By 1920 the widespread use of funeral "parlors" had begun. When people died in institutions the undertaker often brought the body in his ambulance from the hospital to his undertaking parlor, where he prepared it for burial before taking it to the house. Eventually, people decided that the last trip home was superfluous, and they began to plan funerals from the undertaker's parlor. The movement of funerals from private homes to funeral homes proceeded at a slow pace. Undertakers transformed the funeral from a quick committal to a formal affair occurring at an extended interval after death. People supported this specialization of funeral services and the eventual transfer of the viewing to specialized funeral homes.

JIM MELLON

After being discharged from the service in World War I, Manor's "legend" in the funeral business, Jim Mellon, started a mortuary business on the north side of the railroad tracks in the red brick building owned by Thomas J. Miller.

JIM MELLON

Ten years later, on March 30, 1928, he purchased property formerly owned by A. H. Pool along Brush Creek on the south side of town. Jim converted the first floor of the house into a funeral parlor and the second floor into an apartment where he and his wife Margaret lived. Jim Mellon was Manor's first undertaker to own a funeral parlor. He became a friend of the community.

Mellon was an involved participant in the life of the town. He joined the fire department and actively supported his church, Manor Presbyterian. An interesting story about his participation as a fireman is that when the fire whistle blew, it was Mellon who threw the switch. The switch was located in his apartment above the funeral parlor. Because someone was always at the funeral home and the firemen were all volunteers, Mellon and the fire department agreed the fire calls would be taken at the funeral home. They installed an electrical box in his apartment with a switch that was connected to a wire running from the funeral home to two telephone poles and from the poles into the firehouse electrical box. The wire was then connected to the whistle. The telephone number for the funeral home was also the number for the fire department. Mellon received the fire calls, gathered the information, and threw the switch that activated the whistle. He would then call the firehouse and stay on the line until someone arrived to take the call. He also received all emergency calls as he had the only ambulance in town. When he retired, he donated his ambulance to the Strawpump Fire Department.

THE E. J. RODGERS FUNERAL HOME

The lovely white house that is today's funeral home on Race Street in Manor has seen a number of owners since A. H. Pool owned it in 1891. Jim Mellon was the first to own it as a funeral parlor. Since then many undertakers have conducted funeral services from this place. Some readers will remember Jim Gosnell, Lou Miller, and Charlie Russin. In 1961 Charlie Russin sold the funeral home to Vincent Rodgers and his sister Elizabeth. The name of the establishment today is *E. J. Rodgers Funeral Home*. Elizabeth Rodgers has been its owner for 44 years... longer than any of its previous owners. Elizabeth's great nephew, Mark

Bradley, is the funeral director. Mark, like Mellon and the others, lives on the second floor and is active in the community. Elizabeth Rodgers is 94 years old. She lives in Irwin.

Mark Bradley told a story reminiscent of days gone by. Ten or more years ago, during a Labor Day Celebration, an old gentleman stepped onto the porch of the funeral home and introduced himself as "Mr. Pool." He told Mark he was born in that house. He talked about the house and about his family's meat business that was housed in a building situated near the creek. When Helen Sowash was told about this old man she said it was, more than likely, Allen Pool. Allen would be A. H. Pool's grandson, the brother of Ina Pool who taught school in Manor for many years.

Allen Pool is just one example of a former resident being drawn back in time to his old homestead. The house can be included with many of the old landmark homes in Manor.

By Gail Noll and Al Horsmon

JOE CROCK

Joe Crock started working for Jim Mellon at the age of 16. He cut grass, ran errands, and helped with maintenance around the funeral home. His daughter, Joanne, can't remember if her father went to school to become a mortician or if Jim Mellon trained him. But she knows that Mellon employed him for many years. He embalmed bodies and directed funerals. Mellon was the owner; Joe was the director. It was a close relationship that continued until Jim Mellon retired. After Mellon retired Joe stayed on and worked for Jim Gosnell. But it wasn't the same.

In 1945 Joe Crock decided it was time to leave the funeral business and go into business for himself. He and his wife, Marcelle, opened a dry cleaning business in Manor, which they operated for 35 years. In those days, "the cleaner" came to the home, picked up the laundry, and delivered it after it was cleaned. Joe and Marcelle's business was located in the bottom of the building that housed the poolroom. That building today is owned by Joanne Crock and her husband Henry O'Bryan.

By Gail Noll

STONE BROOK MANOR
SENIOR LIVING

In 1985 Mary Jo and Harry Wright bought the house, barn, and six acres of property that once were part of the Rowe Farm. This property is located on Rowe Lane off the Manor Harrison City Road. The history of the farm goes back to the time when the first members of the Rowe family immigrated to Manor from Germany in the early 1800's. The barn dates from the 1860's. The last member of the Rowe family, Leah, died in 1912.

Mary Jo and Harry completely remodeled the farmhouse to create Stone Brook Manor Senior Care, a facility for 18 people. Part of the outside of the farmhouse was the only aspect of the facility that was not completely renovated. Stone Brook Manor quickly gained popularity. In 1995 it was enlarged to accommodate 37 residents. It is usually filled to capacity.

Jane Bollinger, who worked at the bank; Cora Hoyer, who spent many hours volunteering at the Manor Public Library; and Marie "Til" Lauffer, who worked at Westinghouse Benolite, are three Manor residents who at one time made Stone Brook their home. Mary Jo Wright related that while these three women lived at Stone Brook, they all enjoyed being involved in Manor activities.

By Phylis Pietrusza-Levino

MANOR'S LIONS CLUB
"THEN TILL NOW"
SPONSOR
IRWIN'S LION'S CLUB
1948-2005
Fifty-seven Years of Service in the Manor Area

Due to the efforts of seven members of the Irwin Lions Club who were residents of Manor, the Manor Lions Club was formed in 1948. James R. Stewart, founder of the Manor group, contacted Melvin Jones, the founder of Lions Club International, who arranged an organizational meeting for the Manor Lions Club.

Joe Q. Rigney was elected to serve as the first president of the Manor Lions Club and James R. Stewart was elected Secretary, a position he held for many years. Later, James served as historian until his death in 1991. There were 45 charter members.

The first Charter Night of the Manor Lions Club was held on Wednesday, June 16, 1948 at the Penn Albert Hotel's Roof Garden in Greensburg, PA. Three hundred fifty-three Lions and their guests attended. Seventeen different Lions Clubs from the District were represented. The Master of Ceremony was Pittsburgh Pirates' broadcaster, Rosy Roswell. The Vision-Impaired Newcomer Twins from Harrison City, PA provided the entertainment.

For 57 years, the Lions have followed their motto of "We Serve," and have served the communities of Manor, Westmoreland City, Straw Pump, and Adamsburg. Though the primary focus of the Lions is preventing blindness and serving the blind, they are committed to serving their communities and area residents in numerous ways.

MINSTREL GIRLS CHORUS

The development of the Manor Borough playground was the focus of some of their work. Plumbing, electrical work, paving, building maintenance, bridge repair, playground equipment, lawn mowing, and significant financial support were all provided.

Support and aid are given to the local Boy and Girl Scouts. The food banks of the Manor Ministerial, St. Barbara Catholic Church, and Immaculate Conception Catholic Church are supported. Eyeglasses are given to those unable to afford them. Contributions are made to the Manor, Westmoreland City, Adamsburg, and Straw Pump Volunteer Fire Departments. The Manor Public Library, the Manor American Legion, and the Manor-Westmoreland City Community Picnic also receive support from the Lions.

The connection of the Manor Lions Club to the District14-E and International Lions organizations is strong. Focusing on the children of the Manor area, students participate in the 14-E Youth Talent Show and attend the District 14-E Youth Seminar. There is a Leo Club in Manor and a Cub of the Month is selected. The Manor Lions participate in the International Lion's Club Red Ribbon Day Program that discourages drug and alcohol use. The Lions purchase Red Ribbons for the West Hempfield Elementary School, The Harrison Park Elementary School, and the Penn Middle School in the Penn Trafford School District.

Many members attend District 14-E meetings and International Conventions. In 1985, at the Convention in Lancaster, PA, Thomas L. Haubrich was named District Governor of District 14-E Lions. Tom has participated in many District and International projects.

The Manor Lions have financed these many activities by selling Christmas Seals and items made by the blind. They have held White Cane Days, pancake breakfasts, Minstrel Shows, chicken barbeques, and Night at the Races.

Today, the Lions are the world's largest service organization with over one million members. The Manor Lions Club currently has 37 members.

MANOR LION'S CLUB CHICKEN BARBEQUE 1996
Left to Right: Mark Bradley, Jerry Nedley, John Gongaware, Willie Brown (deceased), and Tom Stauffer

By Lion Thomas L. Haubrich

MANOR'S HOCKEY TEAM

MANOR HOCKEY TEAM WINTER 1947-48
Left to Right; Standing: John Greguric, Bob Womer, Brice Heasley, and Bill Fink.
Kneeling: George Heasley and Allen Kukovich held by his father, Albert Kukovich

In the winter of 1947-1948, nearly every town with a nearby pond had an ice hockey team. Nothing was formally organized, but it was a lot like the old sandlot baseball where the best players available from one town would challenge another. There were no officials, blue lines and the goal cages were anything handy, including built up snow. Body checks were frequent but all in fun. These contacts were considered part of the game.

Manor's opponents were mostly Biddle, Oakford Park, Trafford, Herminie and St. Vincent's college players. The Manor Valley Railroad tracks, over the hill where the Ranbar Plant is today, created the pond by holding the water from the area's watershed and several springs. At night, when the coal train from McCullough would slowly pass, the headlight would light up the entire area. This two-minute interval was the highlight of the evening for the skating gathering and the call for "all skate" rang out.

On several New Year's Eve occasions, just before midnight, several fires were prepared at vantage points around the pond. Then just before midnight they were lit. When the whistles began to blow at 12:00 the pond was aglow and came alive with skaters yelling "Happy New Year!" Immediately the feast began…hot dogs, baked potatoes, marshmallows and other homemade goodies. Water was from a nearby spring. These were nights to remember.

By George Y. Heasley

OTHER "POND" MEMORIES

The "pond" remained a place that attracted teenagers during the cold winter months when it was frozen. It has been reported that during the 1950's some students spent a cold day at the pond playing "hooky" from school.

To others, the time spent at the "pond" has been an inspiration. When my family first moved to Manor in 1965, my two older teenage sons enjoyed "pick-up" ice hockey games there. Many times, my youngest son would go along to watch. He became an avid ice hockey player. This interest followed him to high school. During his years at Hempfield Area High School, a school ice hockey team was formed. Today, on cold winter days, teenagers can still be found skating at "the pond."

By Phylis Pietrusza-Levino

MORE MEMORIES

Years ago, merchants did not give customers paper calendars as some do now. Instead, they gave ceramic plates with the whole year on them and name and address of the store. These plates would have the advertising that the merchants wanted the customer to see all year. Sometime in the 1970's Wilfred L. Hepler (former teacher and head cashier at Manor National Bank) was visiting in Philadelphia and saw in the window of a second-hand shop, a Heasley Brothers 1910 calendar plate for sale at $25.00. He purchased it hoping that someone in the Heasley family would want it. When he showed it to Elizabeth Heasley Cox, Dale Cox was there and he was thrilled with it. His mother bought it from Mr. Hepler and gave it to Dale. It is hanging in our dining room today.

Some time later, Eleanor Lauffer Jones died, and then Tom. There was a sale of all their possessions. Among their things was a 1909 Sowash Brothers Calendar plate and Dale and I bought it. I can't remember exactly what we paid for it. It may have been about $35.00. It too, is hanging in our dining room.

These are just some of the little things that people forget.

By Marlene J. (Altenbaugh) Cox

TEEN MEMORIES FROM THE WORLD WAR II YEARS

THE TEEN CANTEEN

The "Canteen" was the place to be on Saturday nights during the "dark" days of WWII. An adult couple, Jimmy Stewart and wife, provided the supervision. A record player was somehow rigged to provide music loud enough for dancing. Tommy Dorsey's Orchestra had recorded its famous "Boogie-Woogie" rendition and the local kids really had the joint jumping. Oh yes, the "joint" was the Manor Fire Hall. There must have been a boy or two who could jitterbug, but the ones who really made the place go were girls like Vella Mae (Maizie) Grieve, Wilma Schott, and the Jones sisters, Alberta and Eva Mae.

Popular songs of that time...who can forget the Ink Spots rendition of *I'll be Around.* Jo Stafford was one of the best loved female vocalists, and Perry Como and Bing Crosby cranked out hit after hit. The Andrew Sisters sang *Boogie-Woogie Bugle Boy* and *Don't Sit Under the Apple Tree.* From England came the songs *I'll Be Seeing You* and *We'll Meet Again.* Vera Lind was the vocalist.

This Teen Canteen should not be confused with "Teen Town." That was an activity that came later after the war years.

SCHOOL EFFORTS

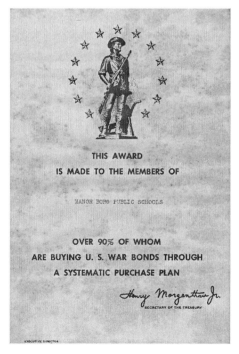

THIS AWARD
IS MADE TO THE MEMBERS OF

MANOR BORO PUBLIC SCHOOLS

OVER 90% OF WHOM
ARE BUYING U. S. WAR BONDS THROUGH
A SYSTEMATIC PURCHASE PLAN

Henry Morgenthau Jr.
SECRETARY OF THE TREASURY

EXECUTIVE DIRECTOR

Savings stamps were sold in school. They came in ten, twenty-five, and fifty cents. You licked them and put them in a book. What you paid for them made the value of the bond, with the ten cents ending up as a $25 bond.

The 9th and 10th grade boys looked forward to getting out of class to go around town on a stake-body truck collecting tin cans and newspapers that patriotic, war-conscious-people had saved. The tin cans were prepared by cutting out the bottoms and the tops, putting them into the can and then stepping on them to crush them flat. This saved space for the can storage. The cans and newspapers were then recycled for the war effort.

THE RAILROAD

The trains seemed to roar through Manor 24 hours a day during the war years. You would see troop trains, flat cars with tanks, and other military vehicles. It was the golden age of the steam locomotives. The train's firemen could be seen shoveling coal into the fiery open doors of the fire boxes as the trains hauled the materials that fueled the war machine. Houses throughout Manor had cinders on their porches that needed swept daily.

RATIONED FOOD

There was a recipe for "imitation butter" that tasted OK. It consisted of a pound of butter, a pound of oleo, and unflavored gelatin. Gasoline, tires, shoes, meat, sugar, and other items were all on the rationing list. Applesauce was used for Crisco. Although it wasn't advertised, these civilian efforts made people on the home front feel that they were doing their part in the war.

THE END OF THE WAR

The Manor fire truck was an old model from the 1920's. It was so lacking in horsepower that when it had to go up a very steep street like Observatory, the driver had to turn around and go up in reverse gear. When VJ Day finally came, somebody got out the old fire truck and we kids jumped on and rode around with the siren going to celebrate the end of the worst war in history.

By Dick Hauser

"I remember VE Day. I was in Clay Avenue School in Jeannette. Whistles were blowing, bells were ringing, and everyone seemed glad. I felt very sad and did not know why. We were all gathered on the steps and hallways and told the war in Europe ended, and we were sent home.
Later, about two weeks or more, we got word that my favorite uncle, Russel McCauley died on May 8th, VE Day. I don't remember VJ Day."

- Phylis Pietrusza-Levino

MINSTREL SHOWS IN MANOR

Minstrel shows were popular among all social classes as a form of innocent entertainment in small towns across the United States and England. Manor was no exception. The Manor Lions Club held annual minstrel shows. These provided the citizens of Manor with a form of entertainment and also provided the Lions with funds to benefit their various projects. The Lions members and several local volunteers sang, danced, played musical instruments, and told good-natured jokes that tickled many funny bones.

TRAINED INTERLOCUTOR VICTOR LOWELL GRIEVE

The performers consisted of an Interlocutor, or master of ceremonies, who introduced the acts. There were actually schools that trained Interlocutors to run minstrel shows. Victor Lowell Grieve, son of Lucien Doty Grieve, often performed in Manor.

There were four "Endmen" two on each side of the stage, who spoke in dialect and provided the comic banter along with the Interlocutor. The chorus was situated between the Endmen and sang songs, including *Dixie* and *Camptown Races*. One of the Endmen would start *Old Kentucky Home* or *Old Man River* with the chorus joining in.

In later years the minstrels added talent contests in the first part of the show. The audience voted and the winner represented the Manor Lions Club in the Westmoreland/Fayette County District 14E Amateur Contest.

Dress rehearsals were held on Wednesday at the Westmoreland Manor, much to the delight of the patients. In return the patients response inspired the performers. The shows were held Thursday, Friday, and Saturday

evenings, always playing to a full house at the Manor School Auditorium. The Saturday evening shows were normally sold out early in the week.

Though the entire show appeared to be effortless, it required a lot of hard work and dedication of all who participated…from the director, to the pianist to the performers. However, everyone involved really enjoyed their experience and looked forward to the next year's show.

By Donna McDowell Nedley

"As well as the Lions Club, other groups were performing minstrel shows. On the next page is a surviving copy of a program that was put on to help raise funds for the Manor Fire Department. Unfortunately, there is only the month of April listed on the program, and not the year. Many will recognize familiar names that were in this performance."

- Phylis Pietrusza-Levino

MINSTREL COMMITTEE

Herbert Schott   Leonard Hoak
William Rigney   Harry McKelvey
Francis Flaherty   Curtis Kooser

ADVERTISING PUBLICITY AND
TICKET COMMITTEE

W. H. Stauffer   J. H. Beamer
T. W. Sproat   H. G. Schott
        C. R. Headley
        C. W. Borland

STAGE TECHNICIANS

J. F. McCurry   C. W. Barton
E. W. Smith   W. H. Stauffer
R. C. Kellner Jr.   E. Richert
        John Elkins

MANOR HIGH SCHOOL AUDITORIUM

April 21st and 22nd

1st ANNUAL

Big Fun Show
and Minstrel

Under the Auspices of
MANOR VOLUNTEER FIRE
DEPARTMENT

Under Direction of
A. G. CARLSON

Music by
IKE SCHEUERLE'S ORCHESTRA

The Booster Club of
Blackville
. . CAST . .

Chas. Augustus Hotfoot .... J. F. McCurry
James Jackson Muchmouth .... J. R. Naley
Hon. Bill Johnson .... J. H. Beamer
William Billkins Smith .... J. W. Cullen
Rufus Rastus Goggenheimer .... F. R. Kornrumph
Abraham Lincoln Washington .... B. F. Cox
Horace Wetweather Cutup .... J. L. Loughner
Alexander Brutus Thicklips .... C. W. Borland
Michael Angelo Wishbone .... L. R. Martz
Garfield Fussfeathers .... F. E. Heasley

TIME—Just before a Political Campaign.
SCENE—Club Room of the Booster Club.

═════

ITALIAN DIALOGUE

Joe .... A. R. Martz
John .... Frank Pink

(Musical Number)

"Where Do You Work-a John" .... Joe and John

═════

SPECIALTY NUMBERS

Dance Specialty .... Miss Jane Kooser
Dance Specialty .... Miss Dorothy Cosgrove

Minstrel
. . CAST . .

Juvenile Interlocutor .... Master Norman Beamer
Juvenile Ends .... { Master Algernon Borland
                         { Master Anthony Call
Senior Interlocutor .... Edward E. Kellner

PREMIER ENDS
Herbert Schott   Frank Cosgrove

PRINCIPAL ENDS
Bus Flaherty   Harry McKelvey
Ray Martz   Leonard Hoak

STEP WITH PEP GIRLS
Dorothy Heasley Edith Anderson Chrissie Grieve
Ruth Gray   Ethel Steffey   Adda Eaton

MINSTREL MEN
Carl Truxal   William Sofko   Arthur Simpson
Russell Schott   William Rigney   Ralph Evans

Minstrel
MUSICAL NUMBERS

Opening Chorus .... Ensemble
"Down by the Winegar Woiks"
.... Juvenile Ends and Interlocutor
"Tonight You Belong To Me" .... Ralph Evans
"If I Didn't Know Your Husband" ....
.... Dorothy Heasley and Carl Truxal
"I Wish I Had My Old Gal Back Again" ....
.... William Rigney
"Give Me A Ukelele and a Ukelele Baby" ....
.... Ray Martz and Leonard Hoak
"I Never See Maggie Alone" .... Russell Schott
"While the Years Roll By" *Quartet* ....
    Herbert Schott, Russell Schott, Carl Truxal,
    Frank Cosgrove
"How Could Red Riding Hood" *End Song*
.... Herbert Schott

Closing Choruses

THE COX AND HEASLEY FAMILIES

The Cox and Heasley families have been strong threads woven into the tapestry of Manor since the early 1900's. They have produced shopkeepers, wood workers, pharmacists, teachers, engineers, and nurses. They have been instrumental in organizing and chairing positions in many of the organizations of the Manor area, such as the fire department and churches.

David Heasley was a coal miner. He married Elizabeth Altman, the daughter of a farmer in Grapeville. They had seven sons but only four lived. Like the father, all four sons were staunch Republicans. Both David and his oldest son Henry saw service in the Union Army in the Civil War. Samuel Heasley, the second son, entered the service of the Pennsylvania Gas Company at the age of 13. He married Sarah Elizabeth Beswick from Penn Township. After 35 years working for the gas company, Samuel retired and held a number of terms as a road supervisor in Hempfield Township. He never learned to read or write, so he kept all his records in his head. At night Sarah Elizabeth would fill in the pay book and figure the men's pay. They had 8 children. Samuel and Sarah Elizabeth Heasley's second child, Charles Rexford (Ford) Heasley was born in 1876. While working at the Westinghouse Air Brake he met a schoolteacher named Florence Balsley. They were married in 1901 and moved to Manor. There, along with Ford's brother Frank, they opened a General Store at the corner of North Railroad Street and Broadway. At that time, the street in front of the store was mud, and a train ran every 15 minutes on one of the four tracks in front of the store. A few years later, Frank opened his own store across the railroad tracks. At Ford's store you could buy anything from shovels and flour to pickles and buttons. Things came in bulk, and Ford would sell them in smaller quantities. Many people "ran a tab" which is like charging things today. The store, unlike many others, survived the depression and remained open into the 1950's. Things changed about this time with the opening of malls and larger more competitive markets.

CHARLES AND
FLORENCE HEASLEY

Charles Rexford and Florence Heasley, seen at left in a later picture, raised 5 children, Elizabeth, Charles, Dorothy, Paul, and Edith. All were active in Manor churches and civic organizations.

During the "hard times" this family was somehow marked by the hobos. These down on their luck people were always taken care of by the Heasleys during the Depression Years.

Charles and some other businessmen purchased property in Rector in 1927. It was known as the Manor Outing Club. When all of the stores closed at noon on Wednesdays, the Heasleys would go there to relax. At that time, traveling to Rector to hunt was like going on a safari today. Travel was much slower on poor roads. The camp shares were passed down within families at first, but that has slowly changed.

Charles R. (Bud) Heasley, Jr. wrote in a family reunion story that Teddy Roosevelt was President when he was born in 1906. Bud got a crystal radio set at the age of 8 and was astonished to hear the news as it happened. He also told that he had to wait for his wife-to-be to graduate from Chatham College and teach three years before she could get married in order to get a permanent teaching certificate. In those times a teacher was not allowed to be married and keep her job. This rule applied to many other jobs then.

FRANKLIN AND MARGARETHA COX

Franklin and Margaretha Cox had four children, Elizabeth, Eleanor, Bertram, and Donald. Franklin Cox left the Westmoreland Coal Company and became a partner at the Irwin Mine Car Foundry Company in Shafton. This was later known as Huwood Irwin. At the age of 50, he retired, but he continued to hunt, and fish. His hobby was making and repairing furniture for his family. His prized pieces were piano benches made of upwards of 50 thousand in-laid pieces.

Margaretha Cox was typical of women of her time. Home and family was their work and, chores were kept to a strict routine, Monday washing, Tuesday ironing, Wednesday general cleaning, etc... Saturday was shopping day, and Sunday was church day.

Sometime in the 1920's, Franklin Cox was asked to make the cabinets for the Dual Tone Victrola. This record player was a forerunner of the later stereo. It used two needles. Franklin joined the business in a factory located along the Penn-Manor Road above the ball field.

For a while business was great, and Dual Tones nearly replaced the old victrola. With the advent of radio, the demand for Dual Tones fell, and the company went bankrupt. The building sat empty until July 4, 1933 when it burned. There is a picture in the 1990 book of this fire. Jake Meyers from Penn bought the site and opened a lumber company.

There are still two dual-tone wind-up victrolas in existence that we know of. One was purchased by Rexford Franklin Cox Sr. of Harrison City at a sale. The second victrola was a wedding gift to Bertram and Elizabeth Cox from Franklin and Margaretha Cox. It remained in their home for many years. Later they gave it to the Manor Outing Club. Many of the records were used as clay pigeons. When interest waned in the victrola, George Y. Heasley, a club member, asked if he could have it. Later, George gave it to Dale Cox. Today, it remains at the residence of the late Dale Cox.

COX FAMILY PORTRAIT 1923
Back row: L-R; Eleanor, Bertram, Bethie, and Elizabeth Middle row: L-R; James Lomicka, holding Bertram Lomicka, Margaretha, Franklin, holding James Lomicka, and Andy Lomicka.
Front row: L-R; Don Cox and Franklin Lomicka.

Babies were still being born at home as late as the 1930's. The doctor came to the home to deliver the baby and filled out the paper work for its name. Babies were often named after family members or close friends, and that hasn't changed much today.

On Saturday, November 14, 1931, Bertram and Elizabeth Cox called for "Doc" Shirey to come to 15 North Railroad Street in Manor. Baby Number 5 was on his way. After the birth, Doc Shirey asked what they were going to name him. The name Dale Clair had been chosen –Dale, after the nice deliveryman who brought bread to Elizabeth Cox's father's store and Clair after Bertram's brother, Donald Clair Cox. Doc wrote the name down as Dale Clare and it wasn't until Dale went to the Air Force and needed his birth certificate that he realized he had been spelling his name wrong all his life.

Over the years there were many mistakes made with the doctor writing down the baby's name.

BERTRAM F. COX FAMILY 1932
Back row: L-R; Lola, Rexford, Elizabeth, and Bertram F. Cox. Front row: L-R; Bertram, Dale, and Audrey

This statement was made about Samuel Heasley, born November 6, 1847:

"Some men as they advance in life lose their progressive spirit and the interest in what goes on in the world, but this has not been the case with Samuel Heasley. Not only does he take note of what passes in his own community and the larger sphere beyond its limits, but he is as eager to reform and advance as the youngest man among us and as ready to "do his lot" in the cause of progress and good government. May our younger citizens follow his example!"

The story on these pages is a condensed version of the Cox and Heasley families history.

By Marlene J. (Altenbaugh) Cox, wife of the late Dale Cox.

THE WILBERT JONES STORY

Wilbert Jones was born in 1921 in a sharecropper's house on the farm of his grandparents in Pitt County, North Carolina. By the fall of 1931 his family was able to purchase a 130-acre farm on Flat Swamp Church Road with the bonus check of $1800 that his father had received for fighting in WWI.

As a child Wilbert attended the Gumswamp Free Will Baptist Church, but was baptized in the Methodist Church in Parmele in 1932. He attended Bethel School from 1926 – 1934 until the 8th grade. Each room contained three grades. As was common in that time, the amount of school attended was determined by the time left over from work on the family's farm. Wilbert's early responsibilities included feeding all the farm animals beginning at age five. Later he had to work in the fields on the tobacco and other crops.

Wilbert bought a car with money he had earned farming a parcel of his father's farm. Because there was no work in North Carolina, Wilbert left for Norfolk, Virginia. There he worked building barracks for the Navy. One day he gave a ride to J. W. Miles, Jr. They became friends and a job was offered to Wilbert by J. W.'s father who was in Pennsylvania. In 1938, Wilbert came to Manor, staying for a few nights with the Miles family. He started at the J. W. Miles Company at forty cents an hour. Wilbert moved to the Manor Hotel first, then to John (Pop) Frye's house on Blaine Avenue in Manor.

Because sheet metal materials were scarce due to the beginning military effort, Wilbert went to Westinghouse Air Brake. He didn't like this work and found a job at the Westinghouse East Pittsburgh Plant. He was drafted in February 1942, but he wasn't called to service until August 1, 1942. This was just before his 22nd birthday. His father promised to save a hog for him until his return.

Wilbert's training was done at Fort Meade, Maryland. He went to Gardiner General Hospital in Chicago to receive first aid training as a medic. He went to Camp Pittsburg, CA where he was shipped to Hawaii in December of 1943. Here, he joined the Seventh Infantry Division. Wilbert was engaged in some of the fiercest battles of the Pacific: Palau, Leyte Islands, Ormoc Bay, and Okinawa, where he had to be hospitalized for 24 days. He received penicillin every four hours for fever during 16 of those days. The division was to go to Japan, but the atomic bomb was dropped on August 6, (Wilbert's birthday) 1945 which led to the end of the fighting. Instead he was sent to Korea in September of 1945 where the goal was to stop the Japanese from invading South Korea. The Russians were invading from the north. The American troops met the Russians at the 38th parallel disarming the Japanese.

Wilbert went from Private First Class to Staff Sergeant (Tech Third) in 1945. He received many war decorations, including five Bronze Stars. Wilbert left Korea and returned to Fort Knox, Kentucky where he was discharged on December 18, 1945.

After his discharge, Wilbert returned to Manor to see Lois Lauffer. Then he went to North Carolina to see his father and the hog that now weighed 500 pounds. After the hog roast in North Carolina, Wilbert returned to Manor.

Bill returned to his job at the J. W. Miles Company instead of Westinghouse because at that time the workers were on strike. In 1961, he and Johnny Vozel, another worker there, bought the J. W. Miles Company. Construction of a new road in 1965 caused the company to move from Wilmerding to Wall, PA. Wilbert retired in 1983, but throughout his career he has been involved in community activities. During his work as a part time officer on the Manor Police Force, he and Leonard Martz, who was the Chief of Police, spent several nights guarding the money that was being moved from the old bank building to the new one. He relayed this event to Gail.

BILL JONES,
MANOR

Her father had never told her this story. Gail relates, "I can just see my dad and Bill standing guard over the tarp covering the money. Bill told me they were two nervous cops, comforted only by their stockpile of weapons."

Wilbert spent 8 years as a part-time policeman. He served on the Manor Council, had a term as Mayor, was again on the Council and served as President of the Council. He has been a member of the Manor Fire Department from 1955 to the present. Bill has served in several offices in the Manor Presbyterian Church. He is a member of the American Legion and the Veterans of Foreign Wars (VFW).

Bill and Regis Holden built the addition to the Public Works Building that now houses the Police Department. The building materials were furnished by Manor Borough; Bill and Regis did the work.

Bill married Lois Lauffer in 1946. He and Lois raised eight daughters. They bought a home from John Naley at 43 Blaine Avenue where they still live today.

By Wilbert "Bill" Jones

BILL JONES,
AT THE NEWLY OPENED
WWII MEMORIAL IN
WASHINGTON, DC.

VETERANS OF FOREIGN WARS IN MANOR

Myron Taylor started the Manor branch of the Veterans of Foreign Wars in 1947. He set up the Manor branch based on the purpose of the national VFW. The goal was to give soldiers a place to meet socially, and serve as

Courtesy - Carl Huszar
ORIGINAL
MANOR VFW
CHARTER DATED
1946

an information gateway to medical assistance and other support that might be needed as soldiers returned to civilian life at the end of World War II. Close communications with VA Hospitals in the area were central to the success of the VFW. In turn, the VFW supported the VA Hospitals.

This organizational idea was not unique to the United States. A similar organization existed in Europe after World War I. Bill Jones' father joined the European group in 1918. The Manor VFW was successful and helpful. The VFW was able to purchase the former Whitehead home located on Trolley Street. This house was used as their meeting place until the late 1950's. The group then moved to Wegley and continued meeting there until they disbanded in the 1980's.

This home was built by Philip Gongaware

FORMER SITE OF THE MANOR VETERANS OF FOREIGN WARS HEADQUARTERS 2005

MEMORIES

The mind holds many memories both pleasant and unpleasant as well.
Some are such sweet memories, while others relate to hell.
Reliving events of a lifetime, announcing the birth of a child.
The fun time of family reunions remembering Mom, as she smiled.
The joy and laughter of childhood, the freedom to run and play.
The reckless excitement of teen years, suddenly shattered by "News" of the day.
The call to defend nations, whose freedom was at stake.
By unjust dictators, who were filled with power and hate.
Torn between family and country, parents and grandparents too.
Reluctant to break that circle of love yet knowing, what you must do.
Shelving the plans that for years were made, casting all dreams aside.
Bidding farewell to your loved one, emotions weren't so easy to hide.
Those years well remembered by veterans who lived through Hell to survive.
Shattered bodies and minds, POWs, MIAs, plus those unfortunate who died.
Recalling "Welcome Home" celebrations the whole nation with gladness resounds.
Yet others recall a somber mood when their "return home" came round.
It's good to have memories for the lessons of life they tell.
To be shared with youth and children becoming part of history as well.
Each Step of the way, is recalled today, with honor, glory and pride.

By Enid Walter

168

THE HISTORY OF THE C. P. LAUFFER FAMILY

Christian Lauffer was born in 1730 and died in 1800. He was called "The Pioneer." He was the common ancestor of the Manor Valley Lauffers who moved to the foothills of the Blue Ridge in Pennsylvania. He had six sons and five daughters. In 1774 he moved to Pleasant Unity. The *Lauffer History* describes the battles at Fort Ligonier, Fort Pitt, and Bushy Run (near Harrison City) in August 5th, 1763. John Sr. was the 4th son of Christian Lauffer and had 14 children. Our *Lauffer History* tells us that John Lauffer, Jr. and John C. Rankin named and laid out the town of Harrison City. Jacob Lauffer was the second son of John, Jr. Jacob had one son, Elijah who had three sons; Clark, Charles Park, and Howard. My name is Vivian Lauffer Horsmon and I am the seventh child of Charles Park Lauffer. I was born in 1926. I lived with my family in a big house on Observatory Street at the upper corner of Fourth Street in Manor. My father, Charles, married Cornelia Yinger.

CHARLES AND CORNELIA 1938

Her father, Brice Yinger, built the large home at the top of the hill now called Breezy Hill Lane off the Manor Harrison City Road. My mother's sister, Catherine, and her husband, Sam Heasley, formerly owned it. My grandfather came to live with my mother and father for his last years. He was a talented gentleman who built many large homes in the Pittsburgh area. On his Manor property, which at that time was in Penn Township, he had an orchard, kept bees, and raised very big rabbits.

When I was born, there were already six children in the family. Eleanor was the oldest; then Ruth and Sarah; then came a first son Ray; and three more daughters, Mary Catherine, Lois Ann and me. C. Martin and James Howard were then born!

Our house had four bedrooms and a hallway that led to our one bathroom. There was a heater in the bathroom in front of a tub that had four feet on its legs. The staircase had a landing with a window, and the living room had a coal-burning fireplace. There was a parlor with a piano. My mother could play that piano from one end to the other. She played every hymn and Sunday school song in her own arrangements.

We were very poor, but didn't know it because my mother baked bread, cakes and cookies, and we had meat, potatoes and vegetables. My father was a great gardener and my mother canned enough for the winter. She even made tomato soup and canned it. We had delicious meals. Every birthday Mother made a big, two layer cake with a wonderful date filling and foamy white icing. I can't remember what we wore, but I remember we got only one pair of shoes per year. We were never allowed to run in our bare feet. We put cardboard in our shoes to cover the holes, and our Christmas presents were new socks and under pants.

I have many memories of the games we played. We didn't have a ball or bat. We made balls out of old socks using the toe with holes. We stuffed that toe with old socks, and then, sewed the open end very strongly. We used our hand as a bat. We played by regular baseball rules, except we were allowed to pitch either underhand or overhand. Also, if you could throw the ball and hit the runner between the bases, he was OUT! We played on the cobblestone brick street in front of our house. The water hole cover on the street was home plate, the telephone pole was first base, anything we could pick up was second base, and a tree was third.

Fourth Street was dirt until they concreted it. If we could find a can, we would step on the middle of the can, with shoes on, of course. The ends of the can would close over the shoe and hold it tight. Then we had a great time pretending we were horses clomping up and down on the concrete.

We were not permitted to leave our block until we heard Scheuerle's Orchestra practicing. Then we could go to the corner of Oak and Fourth Streets and listen to them play.

At night, we played *Run Sheep Run* and *Hop Scotch.* We played cards during the day. We read: the *Horatio Alger* series, *Big Little Books, The Bobbsy Twins, Pearl Buck's* books, a *Law Library Series*, and the *Hardy Boys*, just to name a few. During the school months, the house was usually quiet in the evenings for homework and piano practice, and once in a while, radio listening. Manor School and the Presbyterian Church were our other activities.

Our family and our neighbors were very close. The Hamiltons lived across the street from us. The Sowashes lived down the hill on the opposite corner of Fourth and Observatory Street. The Sowashes had 12 children with only three girls. They owned a food market. The house above ours was where Uncle Oliver and Aunt Katie Lauffer lived. Their children were Billy, Marie, and Dorothy. Uncle Willie, Aunt Katie's brother, also lived with them. Across the street from Oliver and Katie were the Gardners and the Jim Lomicka family. Up Observatory Street were the Butlers and the Franklins. Down the hill from the Hamiltons (their only son Ed was killed in World War II) were the Browns who, I think, had seven children. Next door was Carl Grieve and Vella Meyers. Below them were Jacob and Olive Miller. Their house burned down. I don't know if I saw them jump from their second story window, but I remember watching their house burn down.

My father was a Manor fireman, a charter member of the Westmoreland County Firemen's Association and also of the Western Pennsylvania Fireman's Association. Twenty feet from the upper back corner of our house (the boys' bedroom) we could see Uncle Oliver's garage. The garage caught fire once, and the heat blistered the paint on our house. A horn on one of their cars stuck and blew almost all the time the fire burned. After that incident, I trembled every time the fire whistle blew.

My dad, Charles P. Lauffer, leased the garage next to the funeral home from Jim Mellon, the undertaker. Today, undertakers are called funeral directors. While he leased the garage, he repaired cars and sold gasoline. Many people bought gasoline on credit, and unfortunately, the debts were never paid before he died. During the garage years, I remember cleaning the garage for Labor Day. All the cars were moved to the basement, and the oil and grease drips were scrubbed up. The fireman held a live chicken bingo in the garage, and everyone won a chicken. I remember those poor chickens in the back corner of the garage in wire cages. The Labor Day dances were also held in Dad's garage.

Not many people owned cars in those days, so a Sunday ride with a stop along the way for an ice cream cone was a wonderful treat for all of us. We would sing along the way. On rainy days, my dad would stop at the

school at lunchtime and take most everyone who lived on Observatory Street home for lunch so we wouldn't have to walk in the rain.

We were not permitted to fight in our home, so we were a peaceful family. There was no screaming and yelling. The neighborhood, the school, and perhaps the entire community could

C. P. LAUFFER HOUSE 2005

be called family. This kind of life is

impossible to copy in our world today!

I am not certain of the exact date, but it must have been approximately 1936 or 1937 when our father borrowed money from Uncle Frank Ferree. This money was borrowed to purchase the big old house next to Larimers on North Railroad Street. It had been standing empty for many years with broken windows and a leaky roof. The leaky roof ruined the plaster walls. We moved in and we worked! We had the roof repaired, windows replaced, tore out plaster, and repaired lath strips. I recall George Meckley did a lot of the work for us.

My father first worked at Westinghouse Electric in East Pittsburgh. Then, when the Depression came he worked on the WPA. He also worked at the Westmoreland County Court House and then as a Property Tax Assessor. He was Manor Borough's tax collector for many years. He also helped at Andy Lomicka's butcher shop. They made the most wonderful scrapple. His garden, in later years, used up the entire bottom of the playground side of Brush Creek from the path all the way to the right. He grew every vegetable imaginable. When we finally finished the inside of that 15 room house on Railroad Street, our family life started changing. It seems one by one, we married and moved out. Then my father died, and my mother broke her hip and came to live with Al and me. The house was sold and is now five apartments.

Of all the Lauffer children, only Lois, Mary, and I still live in Manor. Our children all attended Manor School. Albert and I are involved with the community. Al is a fireman and we both are active in the Manor Presbyterian Church. We live in Mount Manor on Observatory Street.

FOUR GENERATIONS
Right to Left: father, Brice Yinger; daughter, Cornelia Yinger Lauffer; granddaughter, Eleanor Lauffer Jones; and great grandson, Welden Jones.

By Vivian Lauffer Horsmon

HARMON LAUFFER - PUBLIC CITIZEN

Harmon Lauffer was raised in North Irwin. When he was a child he vacationed in Manor at the home of his Aunt Emma Berlin who lived next to Howard Lauffer. He married Dorothy Steiner in 1933, and they made their home at the corner of Observatory Street and Blaine Avenue.

NOMINATE
HARMON J. LAUFFER
FOR
MAYOR
-MANOR BOROUGH-

Harmon, better known around town as "Harmy," worked for Westinghouse Electric in the MK3 Department where they made Mercury Arc Rectifiers. His department worked on parts that were used to make the atomic bomb. He worked for Westinghouse for 34 years.

His community service career began around 1940 when Burgess George Grieve asked him if he would accept the responsibilities of Health Officer for Manor Borough. That began his career in politics.

Harmy's wife, Dorothy, was a member of the Jr. Women's Club, and they wanted to use the school for meetings. When he complained to the Manor School Board that social clubs should be permitted to use the building for meetings, he didn't realize that would begin a 30 year association with the Board. He was asked to serve on the School Board to fill the vacancy left by Paul Beamer. He later ran for and won that position. Many in Manor credit his service on the Hempfield Area School Board with making the consolidation work in an equitable manner for all.

Harmy was "drafted to run" for Mayor. He was appointed and served out the three years. When William Thompson retired as Justice of the Peace, Harmy applied for the position and got it. When that term ended, he campaigned for the office and was elected. In 1970 the title Justice of the Peace was changed to Magistrate. Harmon Lauffer was the first Justice to serve in District Court 10-203 which then and now is the magisterial district for Manor, Trafford, and Penn Township.

Harmon Lauffer, age 95, still lives on Observatory Street in Mount Manor.

By Gail Noll

A STORY OF THE
FREDRICK "FRITZ" MILLER FAMILY

My father's name was Fredrick Gustav Mueller, some say Muller, but I remember Daddy telling me it was Mueller. He was nicknamed "Fritz," and our last name became Miller. He was born in Seon, Switzerland in 1878. He came to the United States in 1892 with his grandmother and several aunts and uncles. He was just 14 years old. He spoke no English. The family settled in Larimer, Pennsylvania where he started school. His grandmother took him to school, but because he couldn't speak English, the teacher sent him home. He taught himself to read, to write, and to speak English. In 1899 he became a naturalized citizen. At the age of 21 he went to work for the Pennsylvania Railroad.

FRITZ MILLER AT RIGHT IN DARK SUIT AND HAT

Before working at the railroad, he worked for a coal company in the mines with George Koebler. George invited him to his home one day. It was there he met my mother, George Koebler's daughter, Mary Katherine. Fritz and Mary Katherine were married on May 10, 1901. They made their first home on Third Street near George Koebler's home. When I was two years old, they moved to 27 Broadway Street where they raised their family.

I remember some of the families that lived on Third Street in the early years of 1900: the Steiners, and the Thompsons, Elmer Stewart, the Walkers, Baughmans, Koeblers, Borlands, and Dorothy and Emory Edwards all lived there.

THE HOUSE THAT BURNED

L – R: Aunt Tillie Lewis and Barbara and Mary T. Miller Standing. Mary Koebler Miller's Victrola; Mary Koebler Miller holding Frederick Miller, Grandma Thressia Koebler holding Freida E. Miller, Uncle John Koebler, Uncle George Koebler and Tressa Lewis.

Mr grandfather, George Koebler, fell asleep one night while smoking a pipe. He set the house on fire and it burned to the ground. My grandfather died in the fire.

My grandmother had the house rebuilt and John and Hazel Koebler lived there for several years. Dorothy and Ted Miller, Frank and Alice Koebler, and later Helen and Clair Hanna all lived in the house owned by David and Lois Jones Gongaware today. Fred and Mary Koebler Miller built the house across the street from the homestead. The house next to the Fred Miller home was built by Thressia Koebler Steinbizer. Another home in the neighborhood was that of the Scheibe family. The house on Cleveland Avenue now occupied by Jean and Fred Depp, formerly owned by Margaret Brennaman, was also built by Thressia Koebler Steinbizer.

I remember some of my teachers at Manor School. I remember Sara Sowash being very strict with her brother Moe. Mrs. Shirey used a rubber hose filled with chalk to discipline rowdy boys. Others that I recall were: Ruth Sutter, Mrs. Barrows, Mary Glunt, Alice Wholert, and Ina Poole. Mr. Lemon was the principal, then William Schmidt became principal. I also remember Lucy Stahl and Jane Browne.

Entertainment was a movie at the theatre owned by Rose Zoppetti. We didn't say we were going to a movie, we said we were going to "the show." After the show we went over to Chester "Cheezy" McGuire's for penny candy. Next to McGuire's was King's Ice Cream Store. These stores were next to Flaherty's Hotel.

Our playmates were our close neighbors. We didn't leave the neighborhood. We played with Margaret and Joe McCurry's children who lived below us: Leonard, Charlotte, Walter, Clarence, Clara, and Danny. We also played with the children of Doty and Tressa Grieve.

My parents mail-ordered their food, clothing, and household products from Sears and Roebuck. The order was delivered by train to Manor Station. The merchandise was held at the station until we picked it up. We used small wagons to haul the order up the hill. We bought ten pounds of crackers at a time and cases of canned foods. The soap we used was Fels Naptha. We used it for everything from laundry to bathing and from cleaning to washing hair.

I remember the barbers in Manor when I lived there. There was Nel Simpson, Dick Kellner, Jay Rigney, Mr. Campbell, and the Kistlers.

My brother "Bunty" got his nickname from a nursery rhyme. He liked to hear my mother sing "Bye Baby Bunting." My brother Edward got the nickname "Ted" because he always carried around his Teddy Bear. Then my brother Theodore was born. He was called Theodore, but later in life the identities of the two "Teds" were sometimes confused.

This account was given by Gretchen Miller Lauffer to Gail Noll. Gretchen left Manor in 1947 when she married Clare Lauffer. They moved to Cheektowaga, New York. She returned to the area on September 2, 2000. She is now living at Redstone Retirement Community in Greensburg: Gretchen is 88 years old.

SCHEUERLE BROTHERS

In 1902, Andrew and Antonia Scheuerle immigrated with their three children to the United States from Maravia, Bohemia. After living in Brownsville, Hackley and Penn, they finally settled in Manor. By then, the family had grown to five boys and one girl. Andrew worked in the local coal mine, and Antonia raised her family, took in boarders, and was a local midwife. Music was very important to them. When the boys were old enough, somehow everyone got an instrument and music lessons.

 The oldest son, Ludwig, played violin, but his interest was art. When he was young he had the opportunity to go to Carnegie to study. While in college, he painted the mural in the Manor Lutheran Church. After graduation, he moved to Chicago and became a noted portrait artist.

LUDWIG WITH ONE OF HIS PAINTINGS 1959

Lojas (Ike) and Walter played trumpets, and Rudolph was the trombone player. Andrew, Jr. directed, played drums, and xylophone. He also wrote all the arrangements. In the late 1920's Andrew formed the "Scheuerle (Shirley) Brothers Orchestra" with his three brothers and local musicians. Vaughn Monroe played and sang in the orchestra at that time. There were 12 members and their motto was "Music that Pleases – Rhythm that Teases."

THE SCHEUERLE ORCHESTRA
THE SCHEUERLE COMBO PLAYS FOR AN EVENT
SCHEDULED BY GEORGE HEASLEY.
Left to Right: Andy Scheuerle on xylophone, Bass player is unknown, Harold Easter on saxophone, and Wilfred Hepler on the piano, and George Heasley.

During the 1930's the orchestra played at many of the popular ballrooms in Pittsburgh. They played the Grotto Ballroom, the William Penn Hotel, the Syria Mosque Ballroom, and the Ardmore Gardens among other places. Locally, they performed at the Penn Albert Hotel in Greensburg, the Greensburg Country Club, the William Penn Tavern in Delmont, the Latrobe Mission Inn, and many local VFW's. The orchestra was in demand for proms, senior balls, New Year's Eve, Friday and Saturday night dances, and special

events. Every Sunday afternoon from 3:00 to 3:30 they were featured on WHJB Greensburg radio, and Andrew also played weekly xylophone solo pieces on KDKA radio. Andrew and his brothers were members of the Musicians Union, Local 12.

During the 1950's and 1960's, the orchestra was reduced to 6 members, the 4 brothers with a piano and a saxophone/clarinet player. One of the special dances at that time was at the Manor-Westmoreland City Community Picnic. For many years the people from these communities crowded at the Dance Pavilion at Idlewild Park to listen and dance to the music.

Andrew was asked to direct the Greensburg Musical Society Band. For many years they performed every Sunday during the summer at the gazebo in Ligonier and at St. Clair Park in Greensburg. Rudolph and Walter played, and Andrew directed until his death in 1975.

By Loretta Scheuerle Schroder

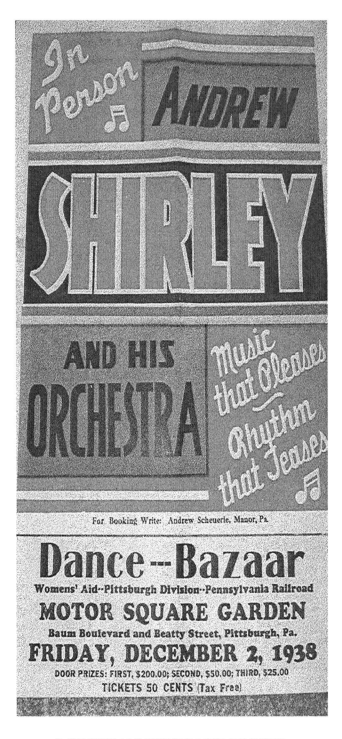

LORETTA'S KEEPSAKE POSTER

SOFKO FAMILY HISTORY

On the eleventh day of December in the year of our Lord one thousand eight hundred and seventy-one, Israel Neleighley purchased Lot #3 on the Manor plan from Samuel Grep of Manor Station. This property lay in the center of North Railroad Street between Lauffer and Mathias homes, and was directly across the tracks from Manor Station. It is now used as a parking lot.

THE LARIMER HOUSE FROM ACROSS THE RAILROAD TRACKS

When Israel Neleighley – over the years changed to Naley – died in 1922, his properties were divided among his three grandchildren: Homer V. Naley, Clyde M. Naley, and Lula Hershey Larimer. Lula received the Lot #3 of Manor, and Homer received the Observatory Street property and one in North Huntington.

HOME OF HOMER V. NALEY, DRUGGIST

Lula Hershey lived on Mount Washington in Pittsburgh until her mother died from injuries incurred one winter when her sleigh overturned. Lula's father remarried, and she was sent to live with her grandfather, Israel, in the house he had built on Lot #3 in the planned town of Manor.

Lula and her husband, John C. Larimer raised their daughter, Lucinda in the home that Israel had built.

Stories were told in Manor of how John Larimer, who lived close to the railroad tracks, would take up the squares of sod in his yard each year, take them out into the street, and shake out the accumulations of black cinders left by the passing steam locomotives.

Lucinda, in turn, raised her three children with husband William G. Sofko on that property. Lucinda Sofko was educated in the Manor School, and returned there to teach for eighteen years. She was active in the Manor Public Library and audited the books in the early years. Her three children, Bill Sofko, Mary Lou Sofko and Jackie McIntyre are still avid readers and today, reside in Greensburg.

LUCINDA AND HER GRANDFATHER, ISRAEL NALEY

The home at Lot #3 was in Israel's family from 1871 – 1976 when co-owners, Mary Lucinda and Mary Lou Sofko sold it to another family. The house has since been demolished.

By Jackie Sofko McIntyre

THE FAMILY OF JOHN "JACK" SPROAT

Jack Sproat's grandfather, Robert Sproat and his family left England for America after the turn of the 20th century. They settled in Manor around 1910. Robert Sproat, his wife Margaret, and five children, George, Tom, Lillian, Polly, and Margaret lived in the last house on Oak Street that is now occupied by the Hensell family. Margaret married James Mellon, who for many years operated Mellon's Funeral Home in Manor.

When World War I began, the United States was not yet engaged in warfare, but Great Britain was. George Sproat, Robert's son, went back to England to join the British Army. There, he met Annie Howarth whom he married after the war ended. They came to America and settled in Manor in the house at the corner of Third Street and Broadway. George and Annie had three sons, Robert H. Jr., George H. Jr., and John, known as 'Jack.'

SPROAT FAMILY HOMESTEAD

Jack tells the story of his father's employment with Westmoreland Coal Company in the Biddle Mines. George had his leg broken in a slate fall. His wife Annie convinced him not to go back into the mines. George went to work for Westinghouse Electric in East Pittsburgh. After only two months, the Depression caused him to lose that job. He found work at McKee Glass in Jeannette where he worked until he was 70 years old. He often had to walk the distance from Manor to Jeannette and back because he could not afford public transportation. When the three boys were of work age, they gave their checks to their mother to help the family. With this kind of support, the family was able to purchase the house in which they lived. George and Annie lived there until they died. The three Sproat boys served in World War II. Jack worked at the Westinghouse Benolite in Manor until he retired. When he started there, T. J. Shrimser and Henry Ball owned Benolite. In 1942 the plant was sold to Westinghouse.

In 1947, Jack married Betty Lee Guy, the daughter of Russell and Mary Guy. They also made their home in Manor where they raised their three sons, Jack Jr., Gary, and Keith. Keith lives in Manor and is employed at the same facility where his father worked, Benolite, which is now owned by the Ranbar Corporation. Jack and Betty Sproat live in Manor at 71 Observatory Street in Mount Manor.

By Jack Sproat.

THE WHITEHEAD FAMILY

Manor Valley Notable

Simon P. Whitehead

S. P. Whitehead perhaps is the best known citizen of the Manor Valley district. Any man who spends 73 years in useful and honorable walks of life is bound to make an unusual mark.

High lights in his career disclose that he shipped his first car load of cattle, from Manor in 1876 to the Pittsburgh market. He retailed as high as 40 head of cattle to the butchers in one week, selling from Jeannette to Larimer. That was in the days before the Chicago meat packers entered the field.

His record as a farmer also is extraordinary. The census of 1900 shows that he raised more grain, hay and vegetables on his farm than was produced on any other farm in Penn township.

Mr. Whitehead is president of the Manor National bank.

In 1905 Simon Peter Whitehead and his wife Elizabeth sold their farm in Penn Township and retired to Manor. Their home on Oak Street is now occupied by the Paul Austin family. The highlights of his career are in the undated news article at left. When he died in 1930, he was still President of Manor National Bank. He and his wife had three sons:

Howard H. Whitehead attended Franklin & Marshall College, class of 1907. He became a successful lawyer. At the time of his death in 1947, he was the Westmoreland County solicitor and President of Manor National Bank. Howard and his wife Clara Elizabeth Mathias Whitehead had two children: Howard M. and Simon Wayne, who is now President of the Manor National Bank.

Charles C. Whitehead, attended Greensburg Seminary. He was employed by Manor National Bank for 55 Years. He and his wife, Martha Jo Mathias Whitehead, had three children, Betty Jane, Charles D. and Nancy Ann.

Simon P. Whitehead, Jr. attended Franklin & Marshal College, class of 1916. He worked for the Pennsylvania Railroad and the Selective Service Administration. He never married and died in 1968.

Submitted by S. Wayne Whitehead

TRIBUTE TO
MANOR WOMEN

By Emily Munson Shirey

Throughout the history of our country, we write history as "his" story.
Often the part the women played in this history is ignored.

We cannot cover every woman and every organization that made
the Manor community a better place to live.

Those included are representative of the many unnamed
Manor women whom we all honor.

HOLLYHOCK ROW

By Emily Shirey

Oh, I like to go a ploddin'
Where the hollyhocks are noddin'
And the bees are talkin', talkin'
All the time I am walkin'
Past that dazzlin' color 'long the old stone wall
I can see the pollen tumblin'
From their legs, so busy fumblin'
Round the yellow clusters hangin' up so tall.
And they stagger with their load,
As they fly on down the road,
With the honey they are makin' for the fall
They are loaded down with gold
But there's nothin' gone – behold!
All that beauty still is noddin' there you know.
Hummin' birds and bumble bees
You may sip just all you please,
Nothing's missed from all that gorgeous flamin' row
Brilliant red and pink and white
All their beauty there unite.
Oh! That garden wall is dressed in every hue.
All the colors God has made
Mingled there in every shade,
Kissed by morning sunbeams,
Bathed in evening dew.

Artwork by Melinda Pietrusza

SARA MORROW WELTY

EDITED FROM THE 1990 CENTENNIAL BOOK

It is seventy-five years since I first saw the town of Manor. At that time it was a village of but two streets with about thirty dwellings, two general stores, one cigar and candy store, two grist mills, a tin shop, and a shoemaker's shop.

My father was a druggist and had the first drug store in Manor. It was in the corner room of the old red brick building at the corner of Race and Railroad Streets.

I shall never forget my first days in the town...(that stretched) along the railroad. It seemed very much like the country – for there were so few buildings – and the woods and fields were so near.

Manor was a town of but two streets, Railroad Street and Race Street. The Pennsylvania Railroad ran through the town just as it still does, from east to west. At the eastern entrance was a sharp curve called "The Devil's Bend" - then the tracks ran straight through until they left the town at the west at another very sharp curve. A number of accidents occurring at this curve had given it that name. There were but two through tracks, and a siding at the Station house. Believe it or not – on the north side of the Railroad the street in front of the houses was wide enough for a farm wagon to be driven on it. For many years the Pennsylvania Railroad kept digging away at the north side bank until nothing now remains of that street except the narrow walk which is still there from Broadway to the eastern end of town. By and by there were three tracks and then four – nothing was taken from the south side of the Railroad.

Manor, which at that time was in Penn Township, was settled principally by retired farmers who had left their homes in the country (to come to) the railroad settlement. Like the stagecoach road of former years, the railroad was the outlet to the larger towns and cities beyond – and was the thing that linked them to an outside world and a wider experience.

I remember the names of all the people who lived in Manor at this time – and know just where they lived. On the north side of the railroad there were 10 dwelling houses, and two little stores or shops. Beginning at Race Street, the first house was the red brick (mentioned before). At this time it was a hotel or tavern, kept by Mr. Fred Klingensmith. The next house was owned and occupied by Mr. H. F. Ludwick. It is now Mr. Charles Lauffer's house. Israel Naleigh lived next – a small shop adjoining his house was at that time a tin shop. Mr. Highberger was one of the early occupants. Later it was a grocery store. Directly opposite the Station House was the home of David Gilchrist.

The last house on that block was Jos. Kline's house. On the corner of his lot was a little candy and cigar shop operated by his son, Fulton Kline. Later Adam Barnhart kept this shop. He was known familiarly to every one as "Barney" and that is where we spent our pennies for peppermint stick candy – peanuts or whatever we could get the most for a cent.

A street which is now called Broadway came next. Across this street was the small frame house of Jesse Miller, now replaced by a large brick building. The next one was owned and lived in by Josiah Berlin. Mr. Berlin owned the house next, which was built by Mr. Schadle, a photographer. In the little frame house next to it – John Barnhart lived. It was later owned by Charles Beswick whose son-in-law, George Taylor, lived in it many years. The last house on the street was the home of Mrs. Rachel Caldwell. Another street started up the hill from there. It is now called Cleveland Street, and that was the end of the town on the north side. East from Mrs. Caldwell's house, on up to the bend where the woods began – there was a green pasture field which we children called the "Commons."

All these houses along the north side of the railroad which I have named were built on lots that stretched back to the alley – now dignified by the name of Atlantic Avenue. Almost all of them had stables, pig pens, coal houses and other out buildings on them. Most everybody kept a cow, and had pigs to kill at butchering time in the fall. All had big gardens, which supplied our tables with fresh vegetables and potatoes enough to last throughout the winter.

We never saw lettuce, nor any other green vegetable until it came from our garden in the spring. I remember when we buried cabbage and beets in the ground, digging them out as needed in the winter. Not much canning was done – seventy-five years ago. I remember the first glass fruit jars that my mother used. Tin cans were used before that. They were sealed with sealing wax. Sometimes when opening a can, some of the red wax would chip off and mix in with the tomatoes for dinner. Folks dried corn – also peaches and apples, and small fruits as raspberries and blackberries. Preserves and pickles were put away in crocks. Nobody every heard of vitamins – nor were we told what we should or should not eat.

I would like you to remember that above the alley there was not one building. It was all pasture land on the hillside. I think it was owned by Mr. H. F. Ludwick. On the south side of the railroad were more houses than on the north. Commencing at Race Street and going east, the first building was the Station House. It consisted of a ticket office and waiting room, freight and baggage room and dwelling rooms of the Ticket Agent who at that time was Mr. J. N. McCartney. Not only was he ticket agent, but he managed all the other business and was also the telegraph operator. Above the station were the stockyards – cattle, hogs and sheep were brought there and loaded on the cattle cars to be shipped east.

Next to the stockyards was Mr. Jesse Miller's Grain Warehouse. I think it is now your Community House. Not only was the grain there in sacks, but great piles of loose wheat lay in parts of the building to be stored later.

A short street separated this warehouse from another old building which was called "the Old Warehouse." This was a big unpainted barnlike structure,…that at this time the farmers brought great bags of wool to the place to be weighed and packed and sent to the woolen mills. The same old warehouse served as a theatre or playhouse in which a number of entertainments were given by the towns-folks. To say that they were amateur is to put it very mildly, but the whole town turned out to see and hear and everybody had a good time.

Close to the warehouse was the home of Mrs. Eliza Walthour. The warehouse was torn down and her house was remodeled later by her son, Mr. Rush Walthour who lived there for years. Small as the town was, (it) had two hotels or taverns we called them. Next to the Walthour home was one kept at this time by a Mr. Heintzleman, later by John Bair. Adjoining this building was a shoe-shop. The Shoemaker was Mr. Alex Bolinger, and it was here we went in the fall …to have our calf-skin shoes made for winter. Next door to the shoe shop was the residence of Daniel Steiner. John Kemerer, who was the village blacksmith, lived next to Steiners, and his was the largest house on this side of the street. Next came another short street, which later was connected to Cleveland Street by an overhead bridge…some of the residents who lived above the Kemerer house – Samuel Gress – John Wanamaker – Jacob Wegley - John Kuhns – James Suter – James Walthour – and Andrew Ramsay, who was a tobacconist and had a small shop there – and that ended the houses on the south side of the railroad. In 1872 or '73 a Planing Mill was built by Isaac Bair – and two more houses were built on the street.

Race Street was so called because of the Mill Race which carried the water to operate Kifer's Mill. Near where the Planing Mill stands, a dam was built on Brush Creek, and the water was turned into this canal or millrace when the mill was grinding. The race came along the street back of the houses on South R.R. Street. When it turned into the lower part of the town at Waugaman's (Now Mellon's) it was then in front of the buildings and was covered by a wooden pavement which ran the length of the street to the railroad where the race went under the railroad track through a small culvert. Beyond that it was uncovered. This pavement was about five or six feet wide, and had side cracks in it – when the mill was grinding you could look down through them and see the water rushing along to the mill. No buildings excepting the mill, Kifer's home, and the small log house which stood on the corner of Kiffer's yard, where Dr. Shirey's house stands were on this end of Race Street. On the north side of the railroad Race Street was seldom called anything but the Harrison City Road. On the South Side starting at the railroad, was the home of Miss Peg and Lucy Bair – Next (to) that was the residence of William Snyder who was an undertaker. Later a store room was built between these two buildings, which was occupied for years by my Father as a Drug Store, after he moved across the tracks from the red brick corner.

The next building (I think)…was a store, kept at that time by James and Ben Portser. There were two stores on that street apart form the Drug Store. They were general stores, for you could buy anything in them from a yard of calico to a horse-collar. Peter Waugaman lived in the last house on the street. Later Mr. Jess Brinker bought a house, which I think is now the Mellon Funeral Home. No buildings except a small house in which lived an eccentric old Englishman, named Tommy Ayres, were on the back street. Later Mr. Rush Walthour built a livery stable there, and I think Mr. Kemerer's blacksmith shop was back there too.

Brush Creek encircled Manor, or rather bounded it on three sides. At the eastern side it crossed the railroad by way of a culvert and was the boundary line between Manor and Tinkertown. The back street I spoke of, was the road which led to Adamsburg. An old wooden bridge which we always called the White Bridge, spanned the creek here and ushered you into Hempfield Township. The creek circled round and not far from the Waugaman house and a foot-log crossed it. On the other side was a row of houses on the hillside which was called, "South Wales." Why so called, I do not know, for I never knew of but one Welsh family living there, and I'm not so sure that he was a Welshman. His name was John Harvey. He was a little man and had such a dialect that one could scarcely understand what he said, so I'm safe in calling him Welsh. Two very pretty houses were on this hill – the homes of Mr. Michael Beamer and his brother, Mr. Jacob Beamer.

And now we will travel but out Race Street from the corner at Railroad Street. The first house was a small frame house in which George Kline, the miller, lived. It was located where Dr. Shirey's house stands, next was the brick house of Mr. Israel Kifer (later the Ludwick home). Across the road was the mill and that ended the town in that direction – with the exception, away out at the turn of the road, stood the school house…

A road or lane came down past Kifer's. It was really just a muddy cow-path, leading from the barn to the street. It is now Observatory Street. About half-way down this lane was a fine spring of ice-cold water. A barrel or tub was sunken in the ground and the clear cold water came out of a pipe into the tank below. Across the lane was Kifer's orchard. Passing the orchard we came to another road leading up the hill. This was called "The hill road to Harrison City." It was not traveled very much as it was steep and stoney, and below this road was a wooded tract which sloped down to Bushy Run, which was a beautiful clear stream of water. An old wooden bridge crossed it here, near the school house. After crossing the bridge the road forked. One fork went west past Mr. Samuel Walthour's house and was called the Sandy Hill Road. The other was the direct road to Harrison City.

Another Grist mill was located near here. The Walthour Mill. This was one of the oldest mills in the valley. History says the first miller there was shot at his door by an Indian. Brush Creek had not much beauty about it as compared with Busy Run for over seventy-five years ago it was a yellow sulfur creek. Yet we youngsters liked to wade in it and play on the large flat stones over which the stream flowed.

There were no walks in the town except for the Board Walks in front of many of the houses and most of these were in very bad condition – with boards missing here and there. As there were no street lights, when one fared forth at night he carried a lantern.

Our water supply was from wells – it was hard limestone water – so most every house had a rain barrel standing under each water spout breeding mosquitoes by the millions – but providing soft water for household use.

After the gas wells at Murrysville were struck we had street lights in Manor. It was extravagantly used and wasted by burning it as it came from a large pipe, with little control at the top of a wooden post, and some times it burned all day, (it) was (a) flaming torch indeed, but was quite an improvement on the old lantern.

A building boom struck the town about 1872 – 1873. Three houses were erected on Broadway – one on the corner of the alley across from where the Presbyterian Church was later built. This house was owned by Mr. Highberger who was called "Grandpap Highberter" by everybody. He lived there with his grandson and granddaughter, Mr. P. H. Naley and Miss Mary Naley. Above this house was the home of another old man Mr. Berlin, who was the father of Mr. Josiah Berlin living on R.R. Street. The third house above was Michael Low's home – our Village Photographer, now the home of Mr. Thomas Miller, and this was, as it still is, the last house on that side of the street, below the school house.

Cleveland Avenue also had begun to climb the hill. Across the street from Mrs. Caldwell's house – a house was built by a Mr. Keefer... Above the alley was the newly built house of Jacob Welty, who had come there from Chadwick farm hear Harrison City. Then James Moore built the two houses above that.

The Methodist church frame building was built in 1873. It was the first church in Manor, and was built at the magnificent cost of $1400.00. The house opposite Mr. Moore's on the corner of Blaine and Cleveland Avenues, was occupied by Doctor J. N. Loughrey who before his house was built, lived in a little old house at the Devil's Bend. I cannot remember when the buildings between the church and Dr. Loughrey's home were built, but it must have been at about the same time as the others on this street.

The old school house, which I mentioned before, was on the outskirts of the town – very near the junction of Bushy Run and Brush Creek. None of my listeners every saw it – but most of you can remember where Mr. Bart Homes' blacksmith shop was located. It was just about that spot that the school house stood. It was a one-roomed shack, unpainted and unplastered – a cold barren room which was supposedly heated by a rusty old barrel stove, which stood in the center of the room. Rude, rough desks and seats with a bench or two, and the teacher's desk made up the furniture. Nails driven along the walls held our coats, shawls and hoods, for believe me, no girl in those cold winter days wore a hat. The place was dirty and unsanitary to the ninth degree. It was so cold at times it is a wonder we didn't all have pneumonia – but aside from the fact that we all coughed and sneezed and sniffled, I can't remember of anyone's having a severe illness.

The school was made up of all ages, from the beginner of six learning his ABC's from a card, to the sixteen year old pupil reading from the Fourth Reader, which was the highest in the Osgood Series, used then. I attended summer session here in 1872, taught by the teacher of the previous winter. He was a one-armed man named David Heasley. The following winter Miss Emma Zimmerman was the teacher. The school was very crowded. In the spring of 1873 Miss Jennie Eccles taught the summer term. She was a good teacher and we all loved her.

In these early days this same old school house was the home of a Union Sunday School, composed of the different denominations in the town. Mr. McCartney, a devout Methodist was the superintendent, and Humphrey Ludwick, a blue stockinged Presbyterian, taught the Bible Class. In the fall of 1873 this old building was burned to the ground...

A lot was purchased on the hillside in town on which a new school house was erected. The present building stands on the same site. It was a two storied, two roomed building. It was late in the season 1873 before it was finished and only one room was completed for occupancy in the fall. The teacher of that short term was Mr. Albert Kepple. In 1874 the upper room was finished and we had now a two roomed school house. The primary room of three grades was downstairs – advanced grades were upstairs. The school faced up the hill to the north. The building was poorly constructed and so frail that when a heavy wind storm came, standing as it did in such an unprotected spot, it would swing and sway so perilously that the teacher would dismiss school for fear of disaster. This danger was obliterated by the placing of two great props – telegraph poles in fact – at the southern corners of the building and that kept us from sliding down the hill. There were no buildings above the school house. Just a sloping hillside at the top of which grew one lone tree – an Oak – which we all called "The Big Tree." A fence separated the school yard from this pasture. In good sled riding weather the most daring of us would take our sleds up to the big tree and ride clear down to Barney's corner. Of course, this meant removing a panel of the fence… Crude as this school-house was, it was a palace compared with the old one, and we were very proud of it. It had a real slate blackboard at one end of the room. (We had only the wall painted black in the old school house) and it had a bell. It was rung by the teacher upstairs. Sometimes, when rung too vigorously the bell would turn over, and then some nimble boy had to be boosted up to the trap door and into the belfry to turn it over. The winter of 1874, Mr. Irwin McCurdy taught upstairs, and Miss Jennie Hodge downstairs. In 1875 we had a man named Wanamaker upstairs who taught only a half term. He was succeeded by Mr. Patrick Wylie. He was as Irish as his name… The next year we had a wonderful teacher and friend. She taught us for two terms, then spoiled it all for us by marrying Mr. J. F. McWilliams. In the year of 1878-79 and '80, my father taught the advanced class – and that finished my days as a pupil then – for the next year I was elected to teach the primary grades downstairs.

Not quite eighteen, with the assurance of youth, and with very little else, I remained there three years, going from there to Greensburg; I might add, too, that I was paid $30.00 a month the first year, which was increased to $33.00 the next years. (I) taught 22 days to the month and walked to Harrison City to get my money.

When I read of teacher's strikes these days for high wages, I laugh to myself, I was the proudest girl in Manor when I was paid this thirty dollars which in those days was quite a lot of money for a girl to earn. I suppose it was all I was worth. I liked the work and if I got results, more than 50% of it was because of that, not because I had any normal school or college training, and the other 50% was just good luck, and my love for little children.

In 1887 this school building was replaced by a three-roomed building. Later as the town grew, other small buildings were built on the school grounds. Then the brick school-house of six rooms was built and lastly the fine building which stands on the site of that one which was built seventy-four years ago.

In those days, very little was furnished by the school board to help us in our struggle for education. In the primary room was a set of large cards on which the alphabet was printed in large type. (You had to learn your ABC's the very first thing of all.) Then there were other cards with such interesting reading exercises as "It is an ax.", "Is it an ax?", "I see an ax.", "It is my ax.", and those poor little six year old children went through that stuff several times a day until they were familiar with one syllable words, then they graduated to the First Reader, which wasn't much better as far as being more interesting although it did have a few pictures in it. Perhaps there was a Primer before the reader, but if so, I have forgotten about it, having been taught to read before I went to school, I never came through this elementary training myself, but I taught it. When we compare this old method with the interesting way in which reading is taught today, we wonder how we ever learned to read. The school board also furnished a set of maps to assist in our geographical knowledge. These of course, were for the advanced grades.

We bought all of our school books – no free writing books, nor pencils. We used our slates for working out arithmetic problems, making pictures and playing puzzles. We did not change text books very often. In all the years I attended Manor school, we read in Osgood's Reader. As we read the selections over and over, they became so familiar to us, that to this day I can repeat most of them from memory. We had Ray's Arithmetic, Berk's Grammar, Goodwich's History, Mitchell's Geography. There was a blue backed speller, whose name I've forgotten. We wrote a copy book, whose fine Spencerian copy never could be imitated. The last year or two of my school-days the study of Physiology was added to the courses and some of us took algebra.

After the Methodist Church was built in 1873, Sunday School and preaching services were held in the new school-house by the Presbyterians. We had a regular pastor by the name of Boyd who was the first minister who preached in the Presbyterian Church which was built in 1877. The third church of the town is the Reformed Church. Rev. Noss was its first pastor, and the fourth is the Lutheran Church. These last two were built after I left Manor.

And now, just a word more. I thank you for listening to this paper. I have probably made many mistakes in some of my statements – failed to properly locate someone's house, which was built in the '80's missed a name or two, but this was not supposed to be (a) strictly authentic history of my old home town. It is just the rambling reminiscences of a very old woman who has turned back the leaves of life and tried to tell you what our old town was like, and what it meant to her in those days so long ago.

Written: June 12, 1947
Mrs. Sara Morrow Welty:
Born: September 36, 1864
Died: March 31, 1950

Edited by Gail Noll

TRIBUTE TO THE WOMEN OF MANOR

A very well known and admired citizen of Manor was Bessie T. (Mc Kee) Walthour. She was born and reared in the Pittsburgh area and met her future husband as she clerked in a store that he visited during his years at the University of Pittsburgh. Bessie and Christopher C. Walthour, a descendent of one of the first families of the Manor area, moved to the corner of Broadway and Atlantic Avenues in Manor after he graduated from law school. He, along with fellow classmates, formed a law firm in Greensburg, PA. Bessie and Christopher had one son, Christopher C. Walthour, Jr.

MRS. BESSIE WALTHOUR

As a citizen of Manor, Bessie was a co-founder of the Manor Public Library. She devoted hours to organizing the library and served on the Board of Directors for many years. Bessie was active in the Monday Evening Club. This club gave women in Manor a place to discuss political issues, focus on the arts, and as a group, they served the community. She also was a devoted member of the Eastern Star.

Bessie's love of children was evident in her vivid blue eyes anytime that she worked with children. She taught Sunday school at the Evangelical and Reformed Church, later known as the United Church of Christ, for many years. She loved to chat with the children when she was volunteering at the library, and she selected only the best in children's literature for the library collection. She was involved with the Children's Aid Society that was a branch of the Westmoreland County Home.

Bessie was known as a devoted wife, mother, and friend. She took great pride in her garden and was known for her culinary skills and her cookbook collection. She has been described as a beautiful, compassionate person who was down-to-earth, soft-spoken, and gentle.

By Dorothy Y. Miller and Helen Sowash

MRS. CORA HOYER

Cora Wissinger Hoyer was born near Johnstown in 1893. After graduating from high school, she clerked in a company store and served as Postmistress of St. Michaels, PA. After World War I, she married Eugene "Gene" Hoyer who had served in the US Navy. Gene worked for the Pennsylvania Railroad, and they moved to Manor to be closer to the railroad. Here they raised four children: Mary Kay, Bill, Jerry, and Thad.

Cora, a good-humored woman who loved a challenge, quickly became involved in the Manor community. She was a charter member of the Manor American Legion Auxiliary. She organized and led their Junior Girl's Auxiliary. Cora was a co-founder of the Manor Public Library and spent many hours volunteering in the library for over 50 years. Every year Cora would be very involved with the Community Chest Drive that later became known as the United Way.

Cora's talents and hobbies were varied. Along with Mary Glunt, she formed a Manor Art Club. She rekindled her interest in painting while in her 80's and explored using various techniques. She also was a professional seamstress. An avid traveler, she and Gene visited almost every state in the nation. When she was 89 years old, Cora traveled to Okinawa and spent several months visiting her son and family and toured parts of Asia.

This independent, accomplished woman was ahead of her time. Cora was an avid reader who modeled life-long learning. She had a gentle way of accepting people. She enjoyed life and quietly encouraged others to excel.

By Nina Miller Kemps

MILDRED LICHTENFELS TARBERT

Mildred "Millie" Lichtenfels Tarbert is the oldest living resident of Manor. She has lived in Manor for 85 years. When she was only 10 years old, her family moved to Manor and bought the home at 25 Third Street. Her father was a railroader, and they moved to Manor from Pitcairn to provide "cleaner air" for her mother who was in poor health. Millie had one brother, Merle, and two sisters, Louise and Jane.

After graduating from high school, Millie attended a business school in Greensburg. She became the bookkeeper for the Shade and Novelty Glass Company in Jeannette. She met and married Jack Tarbert. After living in Jeannette for a short time, they bought the house at the corner of Cleveland and Third Streets that is just across the alley from Millie's family home. Here they reared their two children, Jack Jr. and Jean. Millie lived in this same home until recently when she moved to an apartment located on Race Street.

The lives of the residents of Manor have been enriched in many ways by what this gentle, but firm, woman has given to the community. Millie was very active in the Manor Methodist Church. She held almost every office in the Manor United Methodist Women organization and represented them at many district meetings. Millie volunteered at the Manor Public Library and served on their board as Treasurer for over 40 years. Millie was a Girl Scout Leader for many years. She was their leader in 1976, and many girls remember their numerous Bicentennial Celebration activities. Millie also was very active in the Homemaker's Club.

Millie has been described as, "A woman of outstanding character. She is never self-serving and is open and clear in her communications."

By Phylis Pietrusza-Levino

MANOR PUBLIC LIBRARY

In October 1943, a library committee composed of Mrs. C. C. Walthour, Mrs. E. C. Hoyer, Mrs. John Sofko, Mrs. B. F. Browne, and Mrs. W. Kelly met in the Manor School under sponsorship of William S. Schmidt, Secretary of the Westmoreland County Community Chest, to discuss the possibility of organizing a public library in Manor. The committee was the nucleus of Manor Library Association. Mrs. Walthour and Mrs. Hoyer were elected to represent the committee at the meetings of Manor Community Chest and were authorized to present a budget of $500.00 for the year of 1943 - 44.

A second meeting was held with Mrs. Walthour acting as temporary chairman and Mrs. Kelly as secretary. It was decided that an organization to be known as the Manor Library Association be presented as a subsidiary organization to Manor Community Chest with the five members of the library committee to constitute the Board of Directors: Mrs. Walthour, President; Mrs. Browne, Vice President; Mrs. Kelly, Secretary; Mrs. Hoyer, Treasurer; and Mrs. Sofko, Auditor.

Paul Beamer, President of Manor School Board, was contacted for use of the school library facilities to operate the school library and community library as a joint library. Permission was granted. The library would open every Wednesday from 6:30 to 7:30 p.m. starting October 1944. Two high school students would be appointed to act as librarians and would receive a small stipend. The students would be under the supervision of Mrs. W. L. Hepler, the school librarian.

The library started with 115 adult books and remained in the school until May 1952. At that time, a room with a separate entrance was provided for the public library in the new home of the American Legion. This move in 1952 required some changes to the library system. In the school, the high school students had the protection of the school janitor every Wednesday evening. In the new setting, this protection was not available. Adult volunteers were needed. The public library hours were expanded to Tuesday evenings and Thursday afternoons. The library remained in the American Legion Home for thirty-four good years.

Circumstances and space constraints required another move during February 1986. The library moved just across the street to 57 Race Street that was the Old American Store originally built by Jim Smeltzer during the 1870's. In 1986, it was owned by Mr. and Mrs. John Spicher. The library board signed a lease for the property.

In 1983, the Spichers also had purchased the Old Ludwick farmhouse that was the property next door to 57 Race Street.

LUDWICK FARM HOUSE

As a result of damage from vandals, the unoccupied farmhouse was declared unsafe and a hazard. The Borough had the farmhouse demolished and the Spichers made the property a parking lot.

The move from the American Legion to 57 Race Street was totally accomplished by voluntary community help. Board members, their spouses, sons and daughters, and brothers and sisters all pitched in to make it work. Shelves, desks, tables, chairs, books, and more books had to be moved. Once moved, every thing had to fit into the new space. Shelves had to be adjusted, and all materials arranged. Key to the move and all of the adjustments to the numerous shelves was the volunteer work of Edward (Ted) Miller.

Another volunteer who was extremely helpful was Ruth Larzelere Dvorsky. Both she and her husband were Manor natives who had been neighbors. They were both well educated but had no children. After marriage, they had left the Manor area, but returned as retirees. They had recently moved to the Penglyn Area. After the early and unexpected death of her husband, Ruth continued to live in Penglyn. She was a long time friend of some of the library board members and was adept at organization. During the moving of the library, she was a pleasure to work with, and she felt that she was "home again."

Several years later, Ruth became ill and died. Her will left the bulk of her estate to a college, a hospital, and the Manor Public Library. The library board always dreamed of having a building of their own and had established a separate Building and Equipment Fund. Ruth's endowment added substantially to this account.

About this same time, additional community members became interested in supporting the library. Through the efforts of Enid Walter and a few others, a "Friends of the Library" group was formed. Enid remains a key member with this organization today.

MANOR PUBLIC LIBRARY

Throughout these years, attorney Christ C. Walthour, Jr. advised the library board on how to invest these funds and assisted the library board on any legal matter. Additional donations by community members, including Ethel King, a long time library board member, and Ann Leathers, a founding member of the Friends of the Library, were made to the Building and Equipment Fund. As a result, in 2000 the library board was able to purchase the property at 57 Race Street and the adjoining parking lot from the Spichers. Other building and equipment improvements were funded from this account including: additional shelves and furniture, painting, rewiring the building, remodeling the basement area, and updating the apartments that are on the second floor of the building. In addition, community members have filled a specific library need through memorial donations. You will see small memorial plaques on many items in the library.

At the end of the Twentieth Century, the Information Age and computerization became a major factor in our society. The library board educated themselves on the many ways that libraries work together to meet the information needs of their patrons.

At the same time, the library applied for and received a Bill Gates Grant that completely computerized the library. A common cataloging and circulation system for the entire county was selected. Internet access and purchased online databases are now a part of the library collection. Many of these resources are available via Access PA.

At first, the Manor Public Library under the Library Federation System was part of the Carnegie Library System. Patrons may borrow books from any library in the state via this interlibrary network. Due to changes in the Federation System, the networking location for all public libraries in Westmoreland County was moved to Monessen with many of the library meetings being held at Westmoreland Community College. This change was not well received. The new location is now Murrysville.

The library board learned that to qualify for some of the grant money available for public libraries in the state, some changes needed to occur. A qualified librarian was needed. This happened just prior to the turn of the century. Board members and volunteers continued to assist the librarian and additional services were provided by the library. A library newspaper is mailed to community members highlighting children's programs, special programs, movie nights, new library materials, and calendar of local events of interest. Plans for further expansion of the building were unveiled at the Sixtieth Anniversary Celebration of the library in 2003.

INSIDE THE LIBRARY 2005

Today the Manor Public Library continues to be a source of pride to the Community. Not only are library services provided, but the Library has always been available to community groups for special programs. It has provided space for the AARP Safe Driving Program for many years. A Book Discussion Group was formed in 1995 and continues today, meeting once a month. Some of the public programs presented at the library for the community include: The Civil War, European Travel, Coal Mining in Pennsylvania, Archaeology of Ashkalon in Israel, and many more.

LIBRARY BOARD OFFICERS

President:	Mary Barbour
Vice President:	Darius Markham
Secretary:	Susan Miller
Treasurer:	Helen Hauser
Board Members:	Russell Gadagno,
	Avis Altman
	Dorothy Miller,
	Linda Whitehead,
	Lillian Burkett
Librarian:	Michelle Girardi
Assistant Librarian:	Amy Greshan

By Dorothy Y. Miller

FRIENDS OF MANOR PUBLIC LIBRARY

The Friends of Manor Public Library was organized in 1985 with 63 members.

PURPOSE
To build a bond between citizens and the Library
To create awareness of:
> The Functions of our Library
> The Resources Available for the Public

To help meet the Library Needs
> To Encourage and Promote Support for the Library
> To Encourage the Youth of the Community to Use the Resources of the Library

The Friends of the Library have been able to meet some crucial needs of the library. The Friends were able to provide the library with the air conditioner that was greatly needed. We have purchased folding chairs that are necessary for public programs and meetings. On occasion, the Friends originated special programs for the Community to be held at the library. Our members help with the annual Book Sale held by the library. The Friends of the library plan two fundraisers each year. There is the annual flower sale at Easter. The library is kept open Fridays for this sale. The second fundraiser is a fall bake sale. Friends of the Library are always looking for members of the community to help. New members are always needed.

FRIENDS OF THE LIBRARY FLOAT IN A LABOR DAY PARADE

By Enid Walter

EMILY MUNSON SHIREY

Emily Munson Shirey was originally from the New Alexandria region, and later moved to Manor with her husband, Dr. Charles Shirey, between 1872 and 1873. Emily, her two sisters, and a brother, came from a progressive family. Emily was a school teacher and her brother became a photographer for National Geographic Magazine.

Emily was a very talented and practical person. She has been described as both a ladylike, yet a no-nonsense woman. She was a founding member of the Monday Evening Club and remained a very active member for many years.

Emily was a talented seamstress; although she would tell her friends that ripping day usually followed sewing day! She was involved in Red Cross projects and during the Depression, she and her group sewed clothing for children.

Her artistic ability was well known in Manor. She and her friend, Bessie Walthour, were students of art teacher, Mrs. Charles Steiner. Emily's sketchbook work and china painting were extraordinary. Her works have been on display at programs held in town.

As a school teacher she was always striving to further her education and broaden her horizons. She was an avid reader and maintained an extensive library in her home. One of her favorite books was "The Complete Book of Quotations". I can always visit Emily in my mind when I read those favorite quotes that she checked off in her book. She loved to travel to places of historical interest. She wrote many poems and stories, and some of her articles were published in "Ladies Home Journal." To this day, I recall one of her well written sagas, "The Mills of the Gods Grind Surely Although Extremely Slow."

Emily died in 1940. Her sister, Bertha, was charged with carrying out the instructions of her will: "to distribute all of her personal belongings to her friends." I feel very honored to have been a recipient of some of her special possessions.

Emily Shirey was a splendid example of an independent and talented woman of her day.

By Dorothy Y. Miller and Nancy Miller

VIRGINIA AYRES HOLDEN

1967-1968 PHOTO

The list of achievements this lady has made as a member of Manor Carl Leroy McKelvey Unit 472 Legion Auxiliary is extensive. She has been active since October 1949 when she was enrolled as a Gold Star Sister. Her brother, Gordon W. Ayres, died on December 23, 1944 during the Battle of the Bulge. He is buried in the American Cemetery and Memorial in Luxembourg, Germany.

Virginia's work on behalf of the Auxiliary begins in Manor then moves from the local level of service to the state and national levels. She has held numerous leadership positions and offices, all of which distinguish her as a member of the Legion Auxiliary.

But perhaps the most noteworthy of all her activities are those that might be little known to the public. During World War II Virginia corresponded with 142 servicemen, and since 1987 she has been a Friend of TransAtlantic Children's' Enterprise (TRACE). TRACE is an organization located in England that searches for American servicemen fathers of children left behind after the War.

Virginia has always been keenly aware of the needs of the veterans, and she works tirelessly to provide them with comfort articles. At age 91, she still sews lap robes, trachea covers, wheelchair bags, etc. for patients in the veterans' hospitals in Aspinwall and Oakland. Her favorite admonition to young girls seeking leadership roles is: "Stand up to be seen, speak up to be heard, and sit down to be appreciated."

Virginia lives with her husband, Vince, who in WW II flew 34 missions as a navigator in the 8th Air Force. They have lived in Level Green since 1954. Vince is the oldest son of Manor's former Squire, Vincent J. Holden and Elsie T. Holden.

AMERICAN LEGION AUXILIARY

CARL LEROY MCKELVEY UNIT 472

Carl Leroy McKelvey Unit 472 was organized in May of 1935 with a charter membership of 16 women. Early meetings were held in the borough hall. The highest attained membership was 359 in 1973, and the largest juniors group had a membership of 75.

The Unit was always active in community service, the youth programs, and rehabilitation work for the Pittsburgh-area veterans administration medical centers. Post 472 and the Auxiliary jointly conducts installation ceremonies, hospital parties and entertainment as well as Memorial Day services at nearby cemeteries and the War Memorial Monument in Manor. Hundreds of comfort articles are made and delivered to the hospitals each year.

Annually, a medal award is presented to an outstanding eighth grade girl; attempts are made each year to have the Americanism Essay and Poppy Poster contests held among local school students; the Unit sponsors one or two high school juniors to the Auxiliary's Keystone Girls State Session at Shippensburg University.

A Juniors Group of 23 daughters of World War I Veterans was organized in 1937. Cora Hoyer and Dorothy Schroder served for ten years as leaders of that group. An outstanding project was the collection of 500 books, which became the nucleus of the present Manor Public Library. They also dressed dolls in the costumes of the Auxiliary's Pan American Study Countries and donated books on The Study Countries to the Library.

Post members join Unit Senior and Junior Volunteers on each Poppy Day, and the funds collected are used for the Unit's Rehabilitation and Children and Youth Programs. Funds for the Unit's activities were once earned through the concession at the Post's weekly bingo and banquets.

The Auxiliary ladies cooked and served as many as 500 people every Saturday night for a year. Organizations that held banquets at Manor Legion were: Elliot Company, Jeannette Rubber Works, the Firemen's Association, and Westmoreland County Sportsmen to name a few. The meat was purchased from DelBene's and the food was "home cooked" in the Legion kitchen. Tables were set with linens and volunteers served dinner and poured coffee. Manor Legion's Ladies Auxiliary banquets were high class events that featured savory meals and friendly service. The size of the auditorium was another attraction for large groups. Every inch of space was used. Serving 500 people made service difficult for the volunteers. Banquet numbers rarely fell below 200. Today bingos and banquets are activities of the past for the Legion.

Shut-ins are remembered and deceased members memorialized at memorial services in the Unit and in Westmoreland County Council. Gold Star Mothers were once the special project of the past presidents Parley Committee, honoring them during September each year.

The Unit for many years was in charge of the Mothers March for the March of Dimes, as well as other campaigns for funds in the Manor community.

Manor Public Library, formerly housed in the Legion Home receives donations of books annually...on occasion memorial donations for deceased Unit members...and many individuals and organizations in the Manor Community benefit from the Unit's generosity

In 1935 the Charter members of Unit 472 were: Zeda McVicker, Dorothy Schroder, Chrissie Grieve, Elizabeth Allison, Maude Kornrumph, Elizabeth Lomicka, Marie Kornrumph, Elizabeth Cox, Millie Sproat, Ann Naley, Mary Steiner, Cora Hoyer, Ann Kelly, Ida Rambler, Ada Shafer, and Mary Young.

INSTALLATION OF AUXILIARY OFFICERS 1977
Back Row: L to R. Louise Jasper, Mary Cain, Wilma Selva, and Martha Dawson. Front Row: L to R. Becky Nickle, Ann Sproat, Betty Nicholson, and Virginia Holden.

WOMEN'S AUXILIARY
OF THE VETERANS OF FOREIGN WARS

Similar to the American Legion, a Women's Auxiliary to the Manor Veterans of Foreign Wars was formed shortly after the VFW was organized in 1947. The purpose of the auxiliary was to raise money to help the veterans and to support the local VA Hospitals. In fact, every month a donation was made to the VA Hospitals. In addition, members of the auxiliary would travel to the VA Hospital in Aspinwall to hold "Ward Parties" for soldiers recovering from injuries from the wars.

To raise money, the auxiliary held square dances in the borough hall and sponsored card parties. They also marched in the Memorial Day and Labor Day parades.

When the VFW moved their meeting place to Wegley during the late 1950's, the women decided to hold their meetings in the Manor Borough Hall. Later, they met in the homes of members. The national organization of the VFW disbanded the Women's Auxiliary when the Manor VFW was disbanded in the 1980's.

Past Presidents of the Women's Auxiliary still living today include: Dorothy Kuhns, Mary Katherine Lauffer, and Ruth Durmis.

By Dorothy Anthony Kuhns.

THE MONDAY EVENING CLUB

As the railroads crossed the country, many places became hubs of commerce for the farmers and field workers of the time, taking advantage of the transportation opportunities offered. The town of Manor, first called Manor Station, formed in 1890 from a portion of Denmark Manor in Westmoreland County, was one of these areas.

At this time the town consisted of mud streets, boardwalks, stables for horses or cows, chicken coops, wells, and outside plumbing. There were no streetlights, evening pedestrians used lanterns, houses had gas lamps, not electricity, and the best educational opportunity was in the form of a small wooden schoolhouse.

As the town began to grow and prosper, wives of Manor's leading citizens, businessmen, and professionals saw the need for not only social occasions, but ways to make their town and county a better place to live. At a time when women did not have much access to higher education, places of prominence in the business or political communities, indeed, not even the right to vote, seven original charter members, Mrs. Cameron, Mrs. Wenich, Mrs. Altman, Mrs. Lauffer, Mrs. Williams, Mrs. Shirey, and Mrs. Mathias; formed "The Monday Evening Club." The Club was a place for these women to enjoy not only each other's social company, but a place to further their educations, discuss political issues, gain an insight and appreciation for the arts, and take community action.

The group would meet twice monthly at a member's home. A typical meeting would be called to order by the President, and have the Secretary's report from the previous meeting. Roll call was always answered by mentioning a line item, or subject of the program to be discussed that night. For example: one evening, the program was on "Island Possessions of the United States". Instead of "present", the members would answer "Guam" or "Phillipines", "Wake" or "Midway," and so forth.

Membership was limited to 30, and was not easily granted. A member would suggest the name of a prospect to the group. At the next meeting, a vote would be taken, and ballots counted. If elected, the new member would be notified by the secretary.

Programs would consist of presentations of interesting events of the day; local, state, and national governmental issues. Topics were presented on a very broad scope of study. One year was spent on Holland. Its government, politics, products, and cultures were topics discussed. Many families in town were of German or Dutch descent, and no doubt, many older members spoke the language and observed the customs discussed.

Some other programs included: "Noted Women of Russia" - "The Strange South Seas" – "The Parent-Teacher Association" – "War Foods and Their Preparation" – "Mormonism, It's Origin and Growth" – "An Evening with Uncle Sam – His Joys and His Worries" - "Should Uncle Sam Welcome the Immigrant?" – "Bed Time with the Children" – "Our Unseen Foes, The White Plague, the Hook Worm, and What We Know About Cancer" – One memorable meeting consisted of the members being driven by Clyde Naley in his NEW motorcar to his home west of town.

Club programs show that there were discussions of curfews for the "rowdy boys" who were then upsetting the town; or the problems of the unsanitary conditions of the "holding room," known now as a jail cell, and of the stores in the area who were opening on Sundays. The ladies would discuss solutions to these issues and take them to the Manor Burgesses and ask them to "report fully and enforce the laws of Pennsylvania"

Special projects were done for the Red Cross, sewing was done for the blind, and many clothing drives took place. Clothing was made during WWI and was delivered to families in need.

By 1911 this club had grown to 18 members and 4 associate members. In 1918 an epidemic of influenza hit the country and the meetings were cancelled for several months. The club continued on for years. It spanned two World Wars, and the Depression.

These forward thinking women, The Monday Evening Club, laid a firm foundation for the role of women in the community. Individually, and as a group, they held true to their club motto:

"Think for thyself. One good thought to be thine own, is better than a thousand, gleaned from fields by others sown."

Written by Dorothy Y. Miller

WOMAN'S CLUB

April 1, 1935 – Borough Council Meeting Minutes, Page 161 reads:
"The proposition submitted by Misses Ferree and Hazlett in regard to using the Council Room as a public library and meeting room was then taken up, and after a long discussion by members of council, it was regularly moved by W.C. Gardner, seconded by J.C. Cline, that council grant permission to the Junior Girls Club to use council room as a reading room at their own expense. The motion was carried with H.F. Steiner and W.J. Ehrl dissenting"

A group of young women, some daughters, granddaughters, nieces, and acquaintances of the Monday Evening Club, formed the "Junior Girls Club," which from the Council minutes quoted show their determination to carry on the traditions and examples set by their predecessors who began meeting in 1904. Even though the club never did take advantage of the use of the council room, the group did do some remarkable things.

The Junior Girls Club became the Woman's Club of Manor. Following many of the traditions of the Monday Evening Group, the group met monthly in the homes of members and had similar membership requirements.

The club quickly expanded during the 1940's. The Junior Woman's Club became so large, and had such a diversity of ages and interests, that the club actually split in two in 1949. In fact, at one point there were three different Woman's Clubs in the borough of Manor; The Monday Evening Club, The Junior Woman's Club and the Senior Woman's Club. To belong to the Senior Woman's Club, the member had to be at least 30 years old.

Due to rapid membership growth it no longer became feasible to meet in a private home. The Manor School had just undergone an expansion with the addition of a combined gymnasium and auditorium, and a home economics classroom. Permission was granted for the Club to use the school facilities until the school closed. Various churches were then used until the permanent home of the club became the Presbyterian Church of Manor. As years went by and memberships declined, the three clubs and their members joined together again.

Like it's predecessor, the Monday Evening Club, the Woman's Club of Manor held many interesting programs, meetings, community service events, and charitable drives, all in the spirit of friendship, activism, and fun. There were dances held at the Greensburg Country Club, fashion shows by Gillespies and Ratners, card parties, antiques shows, and Calendar Parties. One fun program was a Bridal Show, not a current fashion show like today, but with each member wearing her own wedding gown or a friend or relative wearing her wedding gown. One member wore a white graduation dress – worn by her own mother in 1912. It must have been quite a great time seeing who still fit into her wedding finery!

The Woman's Club members enjoyed their "Reading Circle". Those interested members purchased a current book or novel from a submitted list. Books were read and at the regular monthly meeting, passed to the others on the list. Books like "Gone With the Wind", or "The Grapes of Wrath" were read and discussed. Many of these Reading Circle books then found a permanent home at the Manor Public Library.

The Club was well known for its charitable donations. There were bake sales and silent auctions along with the regular programs that helped to raise money for a host of worthy causes. The club sponsored Annual Scholarship Awards for outstanding students, and achievement awards were given at Manor School. During the Second World War, war bond drives were held. Members took courses in how to prepare wartime meals, learning how to conserve those rationed and difficult to obtain items like butter and sugar.

Woman's Club members will tell you of their work to support Meals on Wheels, the Community Chest, Torrance State Hospital, Memorial books to the Manor Public Library, local food banks, the Salvation Army, the Boy and Girl Scouts of America, and the Red Cross.

One of the sponsored programs that Woman's Club members are most proud of is the "Student of the Month Award". This award for outstanding achievement at the elementary school level was not based on having the highest grades. Teachers voted on a variety of options each month to select the winner. There were many reasons the award was given to outstanding students, for "Friendship," "Health," "Attitude," "Greatest Academic Improvement," and so forth. Those who became the "Student of the Month" had their names engraved on a brass plate that was added to a wooden plaque. Those former Students of the Month can still see their names on the plaque now at the Manor Public Library.

In their quiet way, the Woman's Club members were always in your midst doing their part, not only to help their community, but to encourage young people to become better educated and to improve themselves, and to learn to accept the responsibilities of life.

The Woman's Club of Manor met for many years, finally having its last meeting on Tuesday, August 15, 1989, due to loss of membership, climbing cost of the Federation dues, the physical ability of the members to assist in fund raising, and lack of public interest. As a fitting conclusion to this community oriented organization, the many pieces of china, serving pieces, silverware, and candlesticks owned by the club were given away to members, donated to a church or auctioned off at the final meeting. Any funds remaining in the Treasury were given to the Manor Public Library and used to purchase their first television, which is still in use today, by the children and citizens of Manor.

CLUB COLLECT

Keep us, oh God, from pettiness;
Let us be large in thought, word, and deed.

Let us be done with fault-finding
And leave off self-seeking.

May we put away all pretense
And meet each other face to face,
Without self-pity and without prejudice.

May we never be hasty in judgement
And always be generous.

Let us take time for all things;
Make us grow calm, serene, gentle.

Teach us to put into action our better impulses,
Straightforward and unafraid.

Grant that we may realize it is
The little things that create differences,
That in the big things of life we are as one.

And may we strive to touch and to know
The great, common human heart of us all.
And, Oh Lord God, let us forget not, to be kind.

By Mary Stewart

ADDED NOTE: Over the years, club membership rolls produced fourteen school teachers, five music teachers, one art teacher.

By Dorothy Y. Miller and Enid Walter

MANOR MUSIC CLUB

ORGANIZED AND FEDERATED IN 1946

COLLECT
We praise and thank Thee, Father, for the gift of music. Through us as channels of Thy Grace may this blessed legacy be shared with all mankind.

Officers:

President	Ann Leathers
V. President	Mrs. Alice Simpson
Rec. Secretary	Jeanne Truxal
Secretary	Julia Selchan
Treasurer	Mrs. Ellen Eaton

The Chorus performed in all the Firemen's Minstrel Shows and the shows presented by the Lions Club. Below are some highlight performances:

1947-48	Music from Around the World
1948-49	Hymn of the Month
1949-50	Performed in Dixie Minstrels sponsored by the Manor Fire Department
1950-51	Sacred Concert presented at Manor Methodist Church. Guest Soloist: Rev. Paul Halstead, Tenor, Sidney Wildman, Baritone, Jean Bennett, Contralto, Margaret Chelsted, Soprano, Organist, Elizabeth Leathers, Guest Pianist, Margaret Gardner
1951-52	Presentation of the play *Dress Rehearsal* at Manor School Auditorium

The Club disbanded sometime after this presentation.

By Marian Painter Eisaman and Enid Walter

MANOR HOMEMAKERS
1967-1991

Homemakers groups were formed by Penn State University Cooperative Extension Service to educate women in the area of family living and consumer education. Patricia L. Long and Nancy Wallace were Extension Home Economists for all 40 Homemakers groups in Westmoreland County. They brought information from Penn State to Westmoreland County Homemakers. Representatives from each of the 40 groups were invited to the McKenna Center in Greensburg to learn new information. Topics such as the proper way to can, freeze, and preserve fruits and vegetables; quilting and needlework were taught. How to create patterns to fit individual bodies was also taught. The Manor Homemakers group, with a membership of about 40, met in the Manor Borough Building twice a month. The activities centered around the information that the representatives had discovered. Pat Edwards set up the tables before the program and helped when we were in need.

Homemakers were a fun group of women who enjoyed a time of learning and doing, not only to benefit our families, but also others. The Home Extension program had a Christmas Fair where tables were set up so all 40 Westmoreland County groups could come together. The ladies displayed the different projects they worked on all year. Crafts were for sale or you could purchase the pattern to make your own. Each group did a demonstration of a particular craft. The Fair was highly publicized and people would come from near and far for Christmas ideas and gifts. There was entertainment and a reasonably priced lunch. All the money collected was used for scholarships presented by the Extension Office to those studying Home Economics, which today is called Family and Consumer Sciences.

The Homemakers Club had special outings. They visited the Smith Glass House in Mt. Pleasant, Westmoreland Dairy, and Linden Hall. They cared for one another by celebrating birthdays, sending get well and sympathy cards. We supported Meals on Wheels, the Lions, and Manor Community Picnic.

Interest in the Homemakers Clubs started to drop off. The group decided to disband. Our account was closed at Manor Bank in January of 1992 with a balance of $37.10 which was sent to the Extension Office for the Scholarship Fund.

By Vera Shale

KAREN BROWN BEYER

The following article was first published in the Tribune-Review on August 11, 2005. The author, Jennifer Reeger gave us permission to reproduce it here verbatim.

HEMPFIELD POLITICAL CLASS TAUGHT LESSON FOR STATE REP. BEYER

By Jennifer Reeger

KAREN BEYER, A HEMPFIELD AREA GRADUATE, IS SWORN IN AS STATE REPRESENTATIVE OF THE 131ST DISTRICT ON AUG. 2 AS HER HUSBAND, MERRILL, HOLDS THE BIBLE.

Karen Beyer can trace her strong interest in politics back to a class she took at Hempfield Area Senior High School. "We got to go to the capital for a couple of days. They had guest speakers. Allen Kukovich, who also grew up in Manor, spoke," Beyer recalled. "I really just sort of took off from there."

Now Beyer, one of the 11 Brown siblings from Manor, has won a seat in the state House of Representatives. She was sworn in Aug. 2 and will represent the 131st district, which spans portions of Lehigh and Northampton counties.

My father was a (Manor) borough councilman and my uncle was a district magistrate, so I've always had a quasi involvement in politics," Beyer said. "But I really got involved and interested in a Project 18 class."

The class, begun by now-retired Hempfield teacher Richard Redmerski, encouraged students to vote and get involved and learn about the political process. "Rich did a really wonderful job," Beyer said. "He did just a tremendous job, and it shows you the result of what one single class can do." Redmerski said he remembers Beyer and her twin brother, Kevin Brown, as good students in the 1980 Hempfield graduating class. "Both of them were very, very, active," Redmerski said. He added it was "exciting" to hear of Beyer's success. "This especially feels good, and it's rewarding to see someone successful in politics," Redmerski said.

Beyer took a circuitous path to the state Legislature. After high school, the daughter of the late Evelyn and Alexander Brown joined the U.S. Air Force. It was there she met her future husband, Merrill, who was a fighter pilot. She attended the College of William & Mary after her enlistment ended and received a government degree while raising her children. Beyer and her husband have three children together. He also has a daughter from a previous marriage. The family moved around a lot during Merrill Beyer's time in the Air Force. "Wherever I lived stateside I got involved with Republican politics just in a kind of informal volunteer way," Beyer said. With her husband retired from the military, the family settled in the Lehigh Valley.

Two years ago, Beyer ran for and won a seat on her local school board. During that time, she worked as a legislative aide for a state representative in the neighboring district. When the House seat in her district came up for a special election, Beyer said several people remembered her for her campaign work. "People knew who I was, and I was asked to throw my hat in the ring and run," Beyer said. The July 19 special election was needed to replace former Rep. Patrick Browne, who had been elected to the state Senate.

During her swearing-in ceremony last week, three of Beyer's siblings, sisters Darlene ad Sharon and brother Will, who all live in the Greensburg area, came to Harrisburg for the festivities. "We're really proud of her," Darlene Brown of Manor, said. "I'm going to get all choked up." Brown and Beyer said they were raised in a Democratic household. "I went into the military and I think military, having lived that life and the life of a spouse, that's probably what changed me," Beyer said. Former President Ronald Reagan also changed some of the family's politics. Some of the children are Republicans, some are Democrats. "We get a little politically charged when we're sitting around having conversations," Brown, a Republican, said. None of the other siblings – who live all over the country – have ever run for public office. But Beyer has run twice and won both times. "I think that's what keeps some people from running, because they're afraid they're going to lose," Brown said. "She has no fear."

Property tax reform, community revitalization and farmland preservation are all issues Beyer hopes to tackle during her term. "The Lehigh Valley is very, very similar to Westmoreland County," she said. "...My values and the values of the folks of Westmoreland County and Manor, they're not too far away from me no matter how long ago I left.

THE FUTURE

It seems that, only when we grow older, do we fully appreciate the stories our elders told us when we were youngsters. Often, we wait until it's too late to capture their memories or identify the people and places displayed in the old photos kept in a box in the attic.

The idea of writing *Manor Pennsylvania, A Place In History* was discussed for many years. Finally, an independent Book Committee made up of 22 present and former Manor citizens, was formed to see the project through to completion. People were chosen who were Manor natives who have the history in their heads. Other contributors were recruited for specific Manor stories. Many of the people on the Committee are third and fourth generation Manor citizens.

People telling their stories bring history alive for the enjoyment and education of future generations. Without a printed record of their experiences and memories, as well as those of their ancestors, their stories would, eventually, have been forgotten and lost forever.

When the committee was asked what word came to mind when they thought of Manor, they all responded in unison: "Home."
And as one member said, "Home is where your history begins."

Just as it was the purpose of the original Manor history book, *The Story of Manor Pennsylvania,* published in 1976, the purpose of this book is to rekindle memories of the past and preserve them for the future. George Y. Heasley, committee member and graphic editor of the 1976 book, expressed that, "Someone should continue the story." No history is ever concluded. A lot of Manor's history isn't in the book; there are many additional stories remaining to be told.

History is the story of people's lives in the communities where they lived and worked. This 2005 book describes what Manor was in the past and what it is today. Hopefully, the next generation of Manor citizens will pick up the cause and document for their descendents, as well as for new arrivals, the essence of what Manor will become in the future.

Bob Cupp and Gail Noll

INDEX

K

L

M